# DIAL 911...

## AND DIE

By
## Richard W. Stevens
### Attorney at Law

**Mazel Freedom Press, Inc.**
**Hartford, Wisconsin**
1999

P.O. Box 270014
Hartford, WI 53027

ISBN 0-9642304-4-5

Distributed by:
**Jews for the Preservation of Firearms Ownership, Inc.**
P.O. Box 270143
Hartford, WI 53027
414-673-9745 — fax 414-673-9746
www.jpfo.org

Cover art by Turner Type & Design, Lacey, WA.

# Acknowledgments

I must thank Aaron Zelman, Executive Director of Jews for the Preservation of Firearms Ownership, for conceiving of this book, urging me to write it, and supporting the effort constantly over the several months it took to finish it. His vision is the reason this book exists. Many thanks also to Marjorie A. Jones, my mother, who read an earlier draft and provided thoughtful critique, suggestions and encouragement. I greatly appreciate the work of Eric Western who typeset and composed the printed text, and Garn Turner who designed the eye-catching cover and prepared the chapter icons. My wife Connie Mariano, M.D., provided the wholehearted loving and financial support necessary to free me to work on the project. Sons Andrew and Jason sacrificed a little time with Dad. And, as in all things, *gloria in excelsis Deo*.

# Disclaimer

Nothing in this book constitutes legal advice or any kind of professional counsel whatsoever. The references, citations, quotations and discussions of statutes and case decisions are for general information purposes only. Although great efforts were made to ensure the accuracy of the information supplied in this book, neither the author nor the publisher can assume any legal responsibility for how the information might be used or the reliance that any person might place on the information. Before drawing any legal conclusions or making any legal decisions in any individual case, a person must consult a qualified lawyer.

All persons who possess and use firearms or any other weapons should learn and practice safe handling techniques. Nothing in this book should be taken as advocating or encouraging any person to violate any law or to commit any crime. Whether a particular action will be considered lawful self-defense depends upon the specific facts and the local law. This book offers no advice about such matters. A qualified lawyer must be consulted for advice in individual cases.

# What Happened When...

- The city had enough complaints to know their chief of police was mentally unstable, but did nothing about him. When the police chief later pulled his service revolver and shot a citizen during an otherwise peaceful traffic stop, could the citizen sue the city for retaining the deranged lawman? *Check out the chapter on Tennessee.*

- Ruth had called the city police at least 20 times in a year, reporting her estranged husband Mack's violent attacks on her and her two daughters. Mack had even been arrested once for an assault. One September day Mack told Ruth he was coming over to kill her. She called the police, but they refused to come. They told her to call back when Mack had arrived. Mack stabbed Ruth to death less than an hour later. Was the city police department liable for failing to protect Ruth? *Check out the chapter on California.*

- Just before dawn two men broke down the back door of a three story home shared by three women and a child. On the second floor one woman was sexually attacked. Her housemates heard her screams and called the police. Their first call to police got assigned a second-level priority and the responding officers did just a quick check and left. The women's second frantic call got a promise of help... but no officers were even dispatched. The attackers kidnapped, robbed, raped, and beat all three women for 14 hours. When later the women sued the city for negligence, did they get their day in court? *Check out the chapter on the District of Columbia.*

- Doctors, neighbors, social workers repeatedly reported suspicious injuries that suggested young Joshua was being abused. The father was suspected; an ex-wife told the police he was really hurting the toddler. The county social worker kept notes, but the agency did next to nothing... until the father beat 4-year-old Joshua so severely that his brain bled and was massively, permanently damaged. Was the county agency held responsible for abandoning Joshua to a brutal household for three years and failing to respond to the mounting reported evidence of on-going physical abuse? *Check out the chapter on Wisconsin.*

# Table of Contents

# Introduction
by James Bovard

Richard Stevens has done a great job of de-fogging the law for average Americans. *Dial 911 and Die* is the perfect antidote for the belief that people don't need guns because the police promise to protect them from everything from terrorists to muggers to things that go bump in the night. Anyone who reads Stevens' book will realize that their right to dial 911 when in imminent peril is often worth less than a plug quarter.

There are many fine police officers in this country. However, both the law and the courts have consistently held that police need not respond to citizens in deadly peril. When the government fails to respond, it is scant consolation that a policeman arrives after the crime to chalk off the body.

## *Punishing Citizens For Government's Failure*

*Dial 911 and Die* goes to the heart of the debate raging over gun control. Gun laws are an attempt to nationalize the right of self-defense. Politicians perennially react to the police's abject failure to prevent crime by trying to disarm law-abiding citizens. The worse government fails to control crime, the more the politicians want to restrict individuals' rights to defend themselves.

But police protection in most places is typical government work—slow, inefficient, and unreliable. According to laws on the books in many states and cities, government has a specific, concrete obligation to disarm each citizen, but only an abstract obligation to defend the citizen. The government has stripped millions of people of their right to own weapons—yet generally left them free to be robbed, raped, and murdered. "Gun control" is one of the best examples of laws that corner private citizens—forcing them either to put themselves into danger or to be a lawbreaker.

## *The King Can Do No Wrong*

Many of the abuses revealed in this book are the result of sovereign immunity. Sovereign immunity creates a two-tier society: those above the law and those below it; those whom the law fails to bind and those whom the law fails to protect. Some of the most shocking cases in this book involve police who wrongfully or maliciously attack private citizens. The fact that government can recklessly endanger people's lives with little or no financial responsibility for the resulting deaths means that the further government control extends, the more citizens will be killed or injured.

Even when the citizen's case against a government agency is not dismissed outright by a judge invoking sovereign immunity, procedural gauntlets insure that fairness will not break out. Because courts treat government agencies—or the statements of government agents—with great deference, private citizens are routinely at a severe disadvantage in any official proceeding.

In other cases, citizens can be required to "exhaust administrative remedies" before taking their case before a judge. And, by sheer coincidence, the agency that wronged them also has the strongest incentive to delay the process on remedies.

## *Pick a State... Any State*

Perhaps the easiest way to start this book is to jump to the chapter on your home state—and then to states of relatives, friends, co-conspirators, etc. Stevens shows that the same defects permeate the laws of state after state. Even in states where the law does recognize that police have some duty to protect specific citizens, court decisions are confused, inconsistent, and offer crime victims little better than a roll of the judicial dice.

Stevens' book is a reminder that there is no substitute for citizens' owning the means to defend their own lives. Even the most advanced cellular phone is no substitute for a good .38 Special.

© Copyright James Bovard 1999. Mr. Bovard is a nationally syndicated columnist and the author of several books including *Lost Rights* and *Freedom in Chains*, both published by St. Martin's Press.

# What the Chapter Icons Mean

 Local courts hold, or are likely to hold, that the police owe no tort duty to respond adequately to a citizen's emergency 911 call for help.

 It is very difficult trying to predict, based on reading the state statutes and case precedents, whether or not a court will hold that the police owe a tort duty to respond to a citizen's emergency 911 call.

 The law may allow the citizen to file a claim or lawsuit against the government (police), but it may be quite difficult both to get a trial and then also prove to a jury that the police were negligent in responding to the emergency 911 call.

 A crime victim may pay a lawyer to bring the case to a jury or bench trial, and the victim has a reasonable chance of proving the case and receiving damages for the negligent response of the police.

# Why I Wrote This Book

It was the most shocking thing I learned in law school. I was studying Torts in my first year at the University of San Diego School of Law, when I came upon the case of *Hartzler v. City of San Jose*.[1] In that case I discovered the secret truth: *the government owes no duty to protect individual citizens from criminal attack*.

Not only did the California courts hold to that rule, the California legislature had enacted a statute to make sure the courts couldn't change the rule.[2] I felt cheated, lied to, duped. And outraged.

All my life I had believed that if the government had one legitimate duty, it was to protect the citizens from aggression. Citizens delegated their right to armed self-defense to the government, in exchange for the government's protection from foreign or domestic enemies of the peace. The Declaration of Independence trumpeted this concept to the world, and the U.S. Constitution and Bill of Rights implemented it in this nation. *Defending the people from violence*, I thought, *was the one thing the government actually had both a right and duty to do*.

Since the founding of the United States, the state and federal governments have greatly expanded their powers. The governments now regulate nearly every aspect of the economy and a huge part of everyday personal life. Licenses, taxes, fees, regulations, requirements, prohibitions, inspections, permits,

---

[1] *Hartzler v. City of San Jose*, 120 Cal. Rptr. 5 (Cal. App. 1975).
[2] Cal. Govt. Code § 845.

zoning boards, mandatory reports and filings—all features of government gone wild. Governments claim to owe a duty to guarantee people food, shelter, income, retirement pay, health, safety, even birth control devices and needles for drug addicts. Some people want government to guarantee or subsidize elective abortion on demand.

Yet the government owes no duty to protect individuals from criminal attack.

It's ironic. It's crazy. It's criminal. As a lawyer, I see why the rule is also understandable. But I could never fully accept the notion, even when I understood all the "good" reasons for the "no duty" rule.

Eight years passed after law school. Enter Aaron Zelman, Executive Director of Jews for the Preservation of Firearms Ownership (JPFO). Aaron's organization published a report entitled "Dial 911 and Die!" The Dial 911 report showed how this "no-duty" rule resulted in terrible tragedies. Defenseless people, at immediate risk of injury or death, had depended upon police response to emergency calls, suffered grave injury or death as they helplessly wait for assistance, and then had no legal recourse or remedy even when the police acted negligently.

Aaron also pointed out the fatal irony: while the government owes no duty to protect citizens, the government is also taking away the citizens's ability to protect themselves. By restricting or prohibiting private ownership of firearms, "gun control" laws work to disarm individual citizens. Making sure that fewer people buy, own, carry, and use firearms is the goal of all "gun control" laws. To see the truth of this statement, consider whether any "gun control" laws *encourage* people to have or use guns. None do.

Aaron Zelman strongly encouraged me to write this book to educate people about the truth which no politician or police chief will volunteer to tell you. In every state of the United States, and in Puerto Rico, the Virgin Islands and Canada, when you call the police, dial 911, and rely on the police to protect you, you are taking a big risk. Under the laws of most of these jurisdictions, the police do not have to respond. They do not have to protect you. In the few places where the law might impose a duty on the police to protect you, the system is appalling: *you (or your heirs) get to pay a lawyer to sue the police after you are injured or killed*. And filing a lawsuit for money damages does not necessarily mean winning... and it does not bring back the dead.

There are thousands of hard-working, honorable police officers in America and Canada. This book does not aim to embarrass these police officers or to tarnish their image. Rather, I hope this book will open the eyes of some of those police officers and their leaders. Lawmakers, media outlets and police officers should not tell people they don't need and shouldn't have weapons to protect themselves, when the truth is that the government (police) usually has no duty to protect individual citizens and too often cannot do it anyway.

Thomas Jefferson wrote that all human beings are endowed by their Creator with certain unalienable rights. Among those unalienable rights are the right to life, liberty and the pursuit of happiness. The right to self-defense is the only way people can protect their right to life and liberty. Free men and women form governments, Jefferson said, to help the citizens pursue happiness with their rights intact. It is hard to imagine a truly free society where the government has taken away the people's right and ability to protect themselves and their families and friends from criminal attack.

We must continually ask the questions. If the government cannot guarantee its promise to protect me, then who will protect me? When the government has taken away my best tools for self-defense, then is my telephone, my burglar alarm or my frying pan going to protect me?

My young sons saw the problem immediately. They said: "Daddy, this is like when the teacher says he will punish you for fighting back in school, but the teacher won't stop the bullies from beating you up. How can that be fair?"

As you read the cases and the laws in this book, ask yourself those same questions.

> Richard W. Stevens
> Alexandria, Virginia
> July 4, 1999

# Brief Summary of The Law

In this book you will read the descriptions of the laws of many jurisdictions. You will come across legal terms and phrases that might not mean much to you. In fact, many of the terms are not fully understood by anyone in the legal system. Lawyers and judges have the job of making sense of the words and concepts, and then applying them in individual cases.

To help you grasp the basic ideas, below is a summary of the law and some brief definitions of the terms you will encounter. This is not a "law book," and it does not pretend to describe every aspect of the legal principles that apply. At the end of this chapter is a list of helpful resources that can assist you to understand the law in this area. To get a legal opinion about the law in any given case or in any given jurisdiction, you or a lawyer must research the particular statutes and case decisions that apply.

The main question in this book is: Does the government owe an enforceable legal duty to protect individual citizens from criminal attacks? In particular, does the government (through its police) owe an enforceable legal duty to respond adequately to an emergency (911) call for help?

## *Duty is the "Flip Side" of Liability*

In this book you will see the terms "duty" and "liability" used almost as synonyms. The concepts duty and liability are directly connected.

In the law, the idea of "liability" is the opposite side of the "duty" coin. If you carry out your duty properly, then you won't be liable. If you don't carry out your duty properly, then you will be liable for damages that your error causes.

Here is how it works: suppose in your state the police department cannot be held liable for failing to respond to a 911 call. In practical terms, that means that the police department *had no legal duty to respond.* Saying it another way, if the police have no legal duty to respond, then they cannot be liable for the damages suffered by the citizen who called them for help.

Similarly, in most states a citizen cannot hold the police (or the parole board or the jailer) accountable for negligently releasing from jail a violent criminal. In legal effect, the police *have no duty to keep a violent criminal in jail.*

Of course in some cases the police department might discipline or even fire a police officer who fails to respond to an emergency call. In those cases, however, the police officer is punished for failing to carry out his or her *duty to the police department.*

In some places there might even be a law that allows the state to bring criminal charges against a cop who fails to do his or her duty. But when the state prosecutes a cop for violating a law, it is prosecuting the cop for failing to carry out his or her *duty to the state.* In any event, internal police discipline and criminal convictions do not pay damages, and they are much too late to help the victim who called for help and didn't get it.

## *Two Ways Government Escapes Liability*

In general, local and state governments cannot be held liable for negligently failing to protect citizens from criminal attack. The reasons vary from state to state, but there are two main ways that governmental entities escape liability.

Government's first shield against liability is "immunity." When a person has "immunity" from suit, that means that nobody can sue the person. To decide whether a person or entity is immune from suit, the courts look at what position the person held or what kind of thing the person was doing. Whether immunity applies does not depend upon whether the person or entity acted negligently or did something wrong. Thus, for example, judges ordinarily are absolutely immune from being sued for their actions in court. A judge is immune because of his position (judge), and it doesn't matter what someone claims the judge did wrong.

The second way governments escape liability is a "no-duty" rule. If the state statutes or the courts say that the police owe "no duty" to protect individual citizens, then crime victims cannot sue the police for failing to protect them. The police cannot be held liable because they had no duty to act in any way different from the way they acted.

In many of the chapters in this book, you will see how different kinds of immunity apply, and how the various "no-duty" rules work in practice. In some cases you will see how the courts use both concepts in the same set of facts.

## *Exceptions to Immunity*

Many years ago, most states enjoyed "sovereign immunity." That idea initially came from the notion that a subject was never allowed to sue a king or queen. Although there has been no king of the United States, the concept of sovereign immunity continued to shield states from lawsuits. The courts believed that allowing citizens to sue the state or local government for performing or failing to perform a governmental function would lead to limitless numbers of lawsuits. Making the government answer in court for every decision and action it took would interfere with the operation of government itself. Government employees would start working to avoid lawsuits rather than serving the common good. The immunity prevented bothersome lawsuits from even being filed.

Starting in the mid-20th Century, the courts began to see things differently. They believed it was unreasonable that victims in car crashes, for example, could not sue the state or city which employed the driver and owned the car that hit the victim. Also, if a person were injured on private property, the person could sue for damages, but not so if the injury took place on public (government) property. The state courts saw this kind of policy as unfair. Many state legislatures felt the same way, but did not want to open up the state and local governments to lawsuits about every possible citizen complaint.

The results of this thinking varied from state to state. Some states enacted laws that preserved sovereign immunity, but carved exceptions for certain kinds of cases, such as contract cases, car accidents, and negligence. Other states enacted laws to repeal sovereign immunity, but then added laws to limit the kinds of lawsuits which citizens could file.

In most states now, citizens can sue the state or local government for negligence. Citizens generally *cannot* sue state or local governments for negligently performing "governmental functions" or "discretionary functions."

A "governmental" function (or duty) is the type of function that typically governments are called upon to perform. A "discretionary" function (or duty) is one that involves making decisions about how to employ resources or what tactics to use to enforce the law.

In most states, planning and policy decisions are "governmental" or "discretionary" functions. Carrying out the duties of a police or fire department are frequently also classified as "governmental" or "discretionary." Under the statutes and case decisions in most states, citizens cannot sue the government for negligently performing (or failing to perform) a "governmental" or "discretionary" function. As you read the succeeding chapters, however, you will see the variety of ways the courts have interpreted these terms in actual cases.

Another term that appears in the law is "ministerial duty." A "ministerial duty" is a task or function that a government agent has no choice but to carry out. If the law requires a police officer to place a ticket on a car parked beside a red curb, for example, then the officer would be carrying out the "ministerial duty" when he or she tickets the car. Some courts hold that a governmental entity, such as the police, can be held liable for negligently performing a "ministerial duty."

Sometimes the situations are complicated. In one case, for example, a county sheriff was dealing with a fallen tree in the roadway a little after midnight when the dispatcher radioed to tell the officer to handle a more urgent call involving personal injuries.[1] The officer left the tree in the road. The dispatcher failed to assign someone else to clear the road hazard or direct traffic around the fallen tree. A motorcyclist hit the tree and was seriously injured. The court held that the fallen tree posed such a obvious and serious danger that the sheriff's office had no choice (*i.e.* no discretion) but to act to reduce the risk. The duty to take care of the fallen tree was a "ministerial duty." The motorcyclist was permitted to sue the county sheriff's department for the dispatcher's negligence in that case.

## *Exception For "Special Relationship"*

The general rule is that governmental entities owe a duty to provide police protection to the public, *but **not** to protect any particular individual*. This general rule is often called the "public duty" rule. The most common exception to the "public duty" rule arises if there is a "special relationship" between the police and the citizen-victim.

This "special relationship" exception in practice operates in the following way. A person calls the police for help, but the police fail to arrive in time to prevent a criminal attack. The caller is injured by the attacker, and sues the police department for negligently failing

---

[1]*Domino v. Walworth County*, 347 N.W.2d 917 (Wis. App. 1984).

to protect the caller. In court, the police argue that they owed no duty to that particular caller, but owed a duty only to protect the general public. The caller then asserts that there was a "special relationship" between the police and the caller. If the court agrees that the special relationship existed, then the lawsuit might go forward to trial. If the court finds there was no special relationship, then the court dismisses the lawsuit. All of the discussion of about a "special relationship" occurs long after the criminal attack or other harm has befallen the victim.

The term "special relationship" does not have just one meaning. Courts have found a special relationship to exist between a citizen and the police, which imposes a duty on the police to protect the citizen, in cases when:

- the citizen is an informer or cooperating witness for the police, and is in danger;
- a court has ordered that the citizen be protected;
- the police voluntarily promised to protect the citizen, and the citizen relied on that promise;
- the police were obligated to warn the individual about the release of a dangerous criminal from custody; and
- a specific statute requires the police to act to protect a class of citizens of which the particular citizen is a member.

Discovering whether there is a "special relationship" is often the key to whether the citizen's lawsuit can go forward against the police, city or state. Whether the facts of a given case will lead a court to find a "special relationship" between a victim and the police will vary from state to state. The variations among the states, and sometimes the variations within the states, make it difficult to know whether the police will owe a duty in an given case.

## *What Is A Tort?*

Frequently in this book you will see the term "tort." The word itself is unfamiliar, but everybody understands the concept immediately. A "tort" is a "civil wrong." A person commits a tort when he wrongfully harms another person.

When a person commits a tort, and causes harm to another person, then the injured person usually can sue for damages. Each of these wrongful acts is a tort: assault, battery, trespassing, false imprisonment, destruction of property, creating a nuisance, fraud or misrepresentation, violating civil rights, slander, libel, negligence, medical malpractice. When a person files a tort lawsuit, the person is usually seeking money damages from the wrongdoer to compensate the victim for the harm suffered.

A tort is different from a "crime" in several ways. A crime is an act that is treated as a wrong committed against society or the state. The government prosecutes an accused person for murder, rape, robbery, and many other crimes. For most crimes, the government must prove its case beyond a reasonable doubt. If the government (the prosecution) wins its case against the accused person (the defendant), then the state punishes that person with fines, imprisonment, or other penalty. Even though the criminal is convicted, in most cases that does not mean that the crime victim receives any compensation for the harm the criminal caused.

In a tort lawsuit, the injured person (the plaintiff) sues the alleged wrongdoer (the defendant) for damages. The wrongdoer might not have committed any formal crime, so there might not be any state prosecution possible. The plaintiff's burden of proving a tort is lighter than the state's burden of proving a crime. The plaintiff in a civil tort action needs to prove his case by only a preponderance of the evidence. If the plaintiff wins a tort case, then the defendant must pay damages to the plaintiff. If the plaintiff loses, the defendant would pay nothing.

Perhaps the most familiar example that will show the difference between a criminal prosecution and a civil tort lawsuit occurred with the two trials of O.J. Simpson. The State of California prosecuted Mr. Simpson for murdering his wife; that was a criminal case. (The State lost). The survivors of the wife filed a civil action for "wrongful death" against Mr. Simpson. That civil case was a tort lawsuit seeking damages as compensation from Mr. Simpson for having wrongfully killed his wife. (The plaintiffs won).

All of the case examples described in this book involved tort lawsuits filed by an injured person, or the estate of the dead person, against the police, the local government or the state. Nearly all of these examples involve claims that the governmental entity was "negligent" and therefore should owe damages for the harm caused by that negligence.

## What Is Negligence?

When a person acts unreasonably under the circumstances and causes harm to an innocent victim, the person is liable to pay the victim for the resulting damages. That simple formula is the basis for the tort of negligence. Using the more formal legal definition, the tort of negligence arises when:

    (1) the person owed a legal duty to the injured victim,

    (2) the person breached that duty,

    (3) the person's breach of duty actually caused the harm to the injured victim, and

    (4) the injured victim suffered actual damages as a result.

To win a negligence lawsuit, the plaintiff must establish each of these four elements. In this book, the question is whether the police owe a "duty" to protect individual citizens against harm. To prove the first element of negligence, the plaintiff must show that the defendant owed a "duty." These two uses of the term "duty" are identical. No plaintiff can win a negligence lawsuit unless the plaintiff can show that the defendant owed a "duty," often referred to as a "tort duty."

In nearly every case, the plaintiff must convince the judge that a tort duty existed. The question of whether a tort duty exists is a question of law for the court. *Juries do not decide whether a legal duty exists. Juries are allowed only to decide by looking at the facts whether the defendant breached a legal duty.* If the jury decides that the defendant breached a legal duty, then the jury must decide also whether or not the breach actually caused damages to the victim and how much those damages might be.

To illustrate how duty works, consider a case of medical malpractice. Such a case is actually just a negligence case brought against a professional. The first element of negligence, legal duty, is present when there is a doctor and a patient. The medical doctor owes a legal (tort) duty to treat a patient with the same degree of skill, care and expertise that is required of a doctor acting reasonably in the same or similar factual circumstances. Once the doctor-patient relationship exists, then the doctor owes this tort duty. With the "duty" element of professional negligence satisfied, the plaintiff then must prove to a jury that the doctor failed to carry out (i.e. breached) the tort duty, and by this failure caused damage to the patient.

When a judge declares that the police owe no duty to protect individual citizens against criminal attack, that decision terminates the injured citizen's lawsuit immediately. The first legal element of negligence is missing. Without the duty element, the case does not go forward to a jury to hear the facts. The injured citizen's case must be dismissed.

## City Liability For Mob Violence

Unless a state law declares otherwise, local governments are not liable for damage resulting from mob violence and riots. Some state legislatures have enacted laws that make local governments liable for the injuries and property damage that mobs or riots inflict upon innocent citizens. In states where such laws exist, however, it is not obvious when a victim of mob violence will succeed in getting a payment from a local government. The victim will first have to file a claim with the government entity, and then if that is not paid, file a lawsuit. A judge might have to decide what exactly is the definition of "riot" or "mob." Must there be a certain minimum number of persons to make up a proper "mob"? What is the difference between a "crowd" and a "mob"? Similarly, a court might have to decide whether property stolen by looters is considered "damaged" for purposes of compensation.

Under the laws of some states, the local government cannot be held liable for riot damage unless the government (police) had some advance notice of the potential for mob violence. The state law might even require this notice be given in writing.

This book does not address the questions of city liability for mob violence or riot damage. A few chapters contain references to laws about riots, but the book does not attempt to catalogue them all.

## *No Constitutional Right To State Protection*

Do the state governments have an obligation to protect their citizens from violence such as criminal attack? Certainly there are several provisions in the founding documents of the republic that suggest the states might owe that obligation. The Declaration of Independence announced the fundamental principle of the United States: all persons are "endowed by their Creator with certain unalienable Rights, [and] among these are Life, Liberty and the Pursuit of Happiness." Governments exist, said the Declaration, "to secure these Rights."

According to its preamble, the Constitution of the United States is intended to "establish Justice, insure domestic tranquility, provide for the common defence, promote the general Welfare, and secure the Blessings of Liberty to ourselves and our posterity." The Fifth Amendment to the Constitution declared that the federal government could not deprive a citizen of "life, liberty, or property, without due process of law." The Fourteenth Amendment limits state government power where it provides that no state may "deprive any person of life, liberty, or property, without due process of law."

In its landmark decision of *DeShaney v. Winnebago County Department of Social Services,*[2] the U.S. Supreme Court declared that the Constitution does not impose a duty on the state and local governments to protect the citizens from criminal harm. Focusing on the phrase referring to "due process" in the Fourteenth Amendment, the Court wrote that

> nothing in the language of the Due Process Clause itself requires the State to protect the life, liberty, and property of its citizens against invasion by private actors. The Clause is phrased as a limitation on the State's power to act, not as a guarantee of certain minimal levels of safety and security. It forbids the State itself to deprive individuals of life, liberty, or property without "due process of law," but its language cannot fairly be extended to impose an affirmative obligation on the State to ensure that those interests do not come to harm through other means.[3]

---

[2]*DeShaney v. Winnebago County Dep't. of Soc. Servs.,* 489 U.S. 189, 109 S. Ct. 998, 103 L. Ed. 2d 249 (1989).

[3]*Id.,* 489 U.S. at 195 (internal citations and parenthetical explanations omitted here for brevity).

The purpose of the Due Process Clause was to limit the powers of state governments, not to impose particular duties upon them. Thus the Court explained:

> Like its counterpart in the Fifth Amendment, the Due Process Clause of the Fourteenth Amendment was intended to prevent government "from abusing [its] power, or employing it as an instrument of oppression." [] Its purpose was to protect the people from the State, not to ensure that the State protected them from each other. The Framers were content to leave the extent of governmental obligation in the latter area to the democratic political processes. Consistent with these principles, our cases have recognized that the Due Process Clauses generally confer no affirmative right to governmental aid, even where such aid may be necessary to secure life, liberty, or property interests of which the government itself may not deprive the individual. []⁴

A state generally cannot be held liable to crime victims under the Due Process Clause because that Clause does not impose a duty on the state to protect its citizens. The Court wrote:

> If the Due Process Clause does not require the State to provide its citizens with particular protective services, it follows that the State cannot be held liable under the Clause for injuries that could have

---

⁴*Id.*, 489 U.S. at 196 (internal citations and parenthetical explanations omitted here for brevity).

been averted had it chosen to provide them. As a general matter, then, we conclude that a State's failure to protect an individual against private violence simply does not constitute a violation of the Due Process Clause.[5]

The *DeShaney* decision largely precludes citizens from claiming that they have a Constitutional right to police protection. There are a few narrow exceptions to this general "no-duty" rule, but it is beyond the scope of this book to discuss them here. Whatever duty the states owe to protect their citizens from crime must derive from state law.

## *References for Further Research*

Most county law libraries and law school libraries will contain all of the following references. Ask the librarian if you are unsure how to locate them.

Restatement (Second) of Torts §§ 314-319 (1965).

53A Am. Jur. 2d *Mobs and Riots* §§ 45-73 (1996).

57 Am. Jur. 2d *Municipal, County, School and State Tort Liability* §§ 441-453 (1988).

63 C.J.S. *Municipal Corporations* §§ 661-669, 673-674, 687, 690-692 (1999)

Joseph T. Bockrath, Annotation, *Liability of Municipality or Other Governmental Unit for Failure to Provide Police Protection*, 46 A.L.R. 3d 1084 (1972).

---

[5]*Id.*, 489 U.S. at 196-197.

Carroll J. Miller, Annotation, *Governmental Tort Liability for Failure to Provide Police Protection to Specifically Threatened Crime Victim*, 46 A.L.R. 4th 948 (1986).

Robert A. Shapiro, Annotation, *Personal Liability of Policeman, Sheriff, or Similar Peace Officer or His Bond, for Injury Suffered as a Result of Failure to Enforce Law or Arrest Lawbreaker*, 41 A.L.R. 35 700 (1972).

Jay M. Zitter, Annotation, *Liability for Failure of Police Response to Emergency Call*, 39 A.L.R. 4th (1985).

18 E. McQuillin, *The Law of Municipal Corporations* §§ 53.04.50, 53.04.60 (3d ed. 1993) (duties of police).

18A E. McQuillin, *The Law of Municipal Corporations* §§ 53.145 - 53.149 (3d ed. 1993) (liability for injuries and damages caused by mobs and rioters).

Gregory G. Sarno, *Inadequate Response to Emergency Telephone Call*, 2 Am. Jur. Proof of Facts 3d 583 (1988) (how to make a case against law enforcement officers and other government agents).

# How to Use The Legal Citations In This Book

Two kinds of legal citations appear in nearly every chapter of this book: citations to cases and citations to statutes. The citation forms generally follow the "Bluebook" format.[1] Using the citations you can locate the legal materials yourself, whether to verify what has been stated in the chapter, or to further your own research.

## *Citations to Cases*

The following case citation is dissected so that you can see how the format works.

**Warren v. District of Columbia, 444 A.2d 1, 4 (D.C. 1981).**

*Name of the case:* Warren v. District of Columbia
*Book in which it is found:* Atlantic Reporter, 2d Edition; volume 444
*Page Number where case starts:* 1
*Page Number where specific material is found:* 4
*Jurisdiction (state or federal):* District of Columbia
*Court:* District of Columbia Court of Appeals
*Year of decision:* 1981

Another example provides shows how the court name is set forth in the citation:

---

[1] *The Bluebook: A Uniform System of Citation* (Harvard L. Rev. Ass'n, 16th ed. 1996).

## City of Galveston v. Whitman, 919 S.W.2d 929, 930-31 (Tex. App. 1996).

*Name of the case:* City of Galveston v. Whitman

*Book in which it is found:* South Western Reporter, 2d edition; volume 919

*Page Number where case starts:* 929

*Page Numbers where specific material is found:* 930-931

*Jurisdiction (state or federal):* Texas

*Court:* Texas Court of Appeals

*Year of decision:* 1996

There are several common abbreviations used for the series of books in which cases are published. They are explained below.

### Federal Cases:

| | |
|---|---|
| U.S. | United States Reports |
| F.2d | Federal Reporter, Second Edition |
| F.3d | Federal Reporter, Third Edition |
| F. Supp. | Federal Supplement |

### State Cases:

| | |
|---|---|
| A.2d | Atlantic Reporter, Second Edition |
| Cal. Rptr. | West's California Reporter |
| N.E.2d | North Eastern Reporter, Second Edition |
| N.W.2d | North Western Reporter, Second Edition |
| P.2d | Pacific Reporter, Second Edition |
| S.E.2d | South Eastern Reporter, Second Edition |
| So. 2d | Southern Reporter, Second Edition |
| S.W.2d | South Western Reporter, Second Edition |

## Citations to Statutes

The "Bluebook" formats for citations to state statutes vary quite a bit, and the variations do not always make sense. Citations in this book approximate the "Bluebook" format. Below is a sample statute citation with its components explained:

### D.C. Code Ann. § 6-2312

| | |
|---|---|
| *Jurisdiction:* | District of Columbia (*not* the federal government) |
| *Type of Law:* | Code (i.e. statute) |
| *Section number:* | 6-2312 (could also be referred to as "Title 6, section 2312") |
| *Book ID:* | "Ann." is the abbreviation for "Annotated" |
| *Ask for the book:* | "D.C. Code Annotated" |

For another example, consider:

### 42 Pa. Cons. Stat. Ann. § 8521

| | |
|---|---|
| *Jurisdiction:* | Pennsylvania |
| *Type of Law:* | Statute |
| *"Title":* | 42 |
| *Section number:* | 8521 |
| *Book ID:* | "Cons." is the abbreviation for "Consolidated" |
| *Ask for the book:* | "Pennsylvania Consolidated Statutes Annotated" |

Another abbreviation frequently used in citations to statutes is "Rev." Thus you might see:

**Or. Rev. Stat. Ann. § 30.265.**

This refers to the book series entitled "Oregon Revised Statutes Annotated."

Any law librarian can help you find the materials cited in this book using the citations provided in the footnotes.

# State of Alabama

The Alabama constitution and statutes shield the state, as well as state sheriffs and city police officers, from liability for their "discretionary decision-making functions."[1] A city in Alabama can be sued for negligence, however, unless a court decides that holding the city liable would "materially thwart the City's legitimate efforts to provide [essential] public services."[2]

Under the rule, one city was not liable for supplying *only* 82 police officers to keep the peace at a stadium fireworks display, when those officers were unable to prevent gang attacks on individuals at the stadium during the event.[3] On the other hand, when a city police officer was already on the scene of a crime but failed to act reasonably under the circumstances, that city was held liable.[4] The difference between the cases was that the courts do not want lawsuits to interfere with how the police departments decide to assign

---

[1] *Rose v. Town of Jackson's Gap*, 952 F. Supp. 757, 766-67 & n.13 (M.D. Ala. 1996), *citing* Alabama Code § 6-5-338 (immunizing state and municipal peace officers from tort liability); *Drain v. Odom*, 631 So. 2d 971, 972 (Ala. 1994)(sheriffs and their deputies are executive officers of the state and thus are immune from negligence suits), *citing* Alabama Const. of 1901 Art. I, § 14.

[2] *City of Birmingham v. Benson*, 631 So. 2d 902, 904 (Ala. 1993), *quoting Rich v. City of Mobile*, 410 So. 2d 385, 387-88 (Ala. 1982)(internal quotation and citations omitted).

[3] *Benson*, 631 So. 2d at 905, *citing Garrett v. City of Mobile*, 481 So. 2d 376, 377 (Ala. 1985).

[4] *Benson*, 631 So. 2d at 905, *citing, inter alia, Luker v. City of Branley*, 520 So. 2d 517 (Ala. 1987).

officers, but the courts will allow suits when the individual police officer is negligent.

## *Defenseless Boy Dies... City Pays*

Officer Vining, a Birmingham policeman, was working as a part-time security guard at a bar in town.[5] Officer Vining was guarding at the bar on December 14, 1990. He was in full police uniform with radio, gun, nightstick, flashlight, handcuffs and mace. At the bar many minors were illegally buying liquor. That night, two young men got into trouble; one died.

Billy Weidler threatened Blair Benson in the bar. Blair asked Officer Vining to escort him and three other minors with him to their car. Vining told the men they could not fight in the bar, and did escort Blair and the others outside. A crowd followed them onto the sidewalk. Vining stood on the sidewalk as Blair and his party crossed the street. The young man who had threatened Blair, Billy Weidler, asked Vining what he was going to do. Officer Vining told Weidler, "I don't care what you do, I am going back inside."

Moments later, Weidler and a crowd of over 15 youths chased Blair and the others, pulled Blair out of the car and beat him for 5 to 10 minutes. Blair was knocked down, kicked, and run over by the car in which his friends were trying to leave. Blair died of his injuries. Weidler and another youth were convicted of manslaughter.

Blair's father sued the city and Officer Vining. The jury awarded him $1.6 million in damages. The

---

[5]The facts and law of this case are set forth in *City of Birmingham v. Benson*, 631 So. 2d 902 (Ala. 1993).

Supreme Court of Alabama upheld the award. Because the officer was on the scene at the time the victim and the aggressor were also present, the Court was unwilling to immunize the officer or the city from liability. The fully-armed officer could easily have prevented the horrendous crime but did not. Instead, the officer practically encouraged Weidler to hurt Blair. The Court held that the city and the officer should face liability under the legal principles that apply to other negligence cases.

When the legal smoke had cleared, Blair was still dead. His father received a large money award. His father's lawyers doubtless received a large fee well-earned. Still, might Blair be alive today had he, or any one of his friends, been able to brandish a firearm at the vicious attackers in the crowd?

# State of Alaska

The law is puzzling in Alaska. Two statutes seem to both allow and preclude citizens from suing the government. First there is the statute which allows citizens to sue the state for personal injury and property damage claims.[1] The same statute also carries an exception for cases where the citizen is suing the state because one of its employees was negligent. The statute provides that "no action may be brought" if the citizen's claim "is an action for tort, and based upon the exercise or performance or the failure to exercise or perform a discretionary function or duty on the part of a state agency... whether or not the discretion involved is abused."[2]

Another statute allows citizens to sue the city government.[3] Just like the statute that applies to the state government, this statute precludes citizens from suing the city when their employees are negligent in the performance of "discretionary" functions or duties.[4] Under the law in many states, responding to police emergency calls is a "discretionary" function. These Alaska statutes seem to give immunity to the police departments, and thereby prevent citizens from suing police for failing to protect them.

Curiously, the Supreme Court of Alaska has held, in *City of Kotzebue v. McLean*,[5] that the city could be sued

---

[1] Alaska Stat. § 09.50.250.

[2] Alaska Stat. § 09.50.250(1).

[3] Alaska Stat. § 09.65.070.

[4] Alaska Stat. § 09.65.070(d)(2).

[5] *City of Kotzebue v. McLean*, 702 P.2d 1309 (Alaska 1985).

like anybody else for negligently mishandling an emergency call. The Court expressly ignored the statutes in that case and refused to consider the city's claim that it was immune from suit. Why? Because the city's lawyers failed to make the statutory immunity argument in their initial brief to the Court.[6]

The Court did consider the "public duty" rule, however, and rejected it. Under that rule, the city police owe a duty to protect the public, but not to protect any specific individual, unless there is a "special relationship" between the police and that individual. The Alaska Court held that the "public duty" rule does not apply in that state.

Because the *City of Kotzebue* decision was made without considering the controlling Alaska statutes, lawyers and trial court judges cannot be sure whether the state's high court would allow a citizen to sue the city or state in a future "dial 911" case. Being so uncertain in the law gives lawyers headaches, but should also give citizens pause. Do police owe a duty to respond to emergencies calls or not?

## *Just Let Me Finish My Paperwork First*

Billy Howarth called the Kotzebue police station at 2:45 a.m. on March 12, 1977.[7] Howarth gave his name, said generally where he was, and announced that "he was going to kill a friend of his." The location was just a few minutes away from the police station.

---

[6]*Id.*, 702 P.2d at 1312 & n.2.

[7]The facts and law of this case are set forth in *City of Kotzebue v. McLean,* 702 P.2d 1309 (Alaska 1985).

The police officer who received Howarth's call was busy at the moment. He was processing the paperwork for a drunk minor whom the officer had just arrested. Although others were available at the station who could have watched the minor while the officer checked on the call, the officer decided to finish filling out the papers before responding to the call. The officer knew that an off-duty cop was working as a security guard very near Howarth's location, but the officer took no steps to contact that guard.

Twelve minutes later, at 2:57 a.m., the officer responded to the call and arrived on the scene at 3:00 a.m. By then Howarth had already stabbed Douglas McLean. The officer found McLean lying in his own blood on the floor of the hotel bar.

McLean sued the city for negligently failing to respond to Howarth's clear threat to kill, which Howarth himself had phoned into the police. McLean's case went to trial. The jury found the police to be negligent and awarded McLean $180,000 in damages.

After rejecting the "public duty" rule and ignoring the statutes on the books (as discussed above), the Supreme Court of Alaska in 1985 upheld the jury award. Yet the law in Alaska remains unclear. If an officer is snowed under by paperwork at the police station, will the officer's first duty be to answer your call for help?

Do you want to find out?

# State of Arizona

On the question of government tort duty and liability, Arizona law has undergone a number of changes over recent years.[1] One key question is whether a city can be sued when its 911 operator negligently handles an emergency call. The answer is "yes." In 1998, the Supreme Court of Arizona affirmed a net judgment of $1,275,000 against the City of Phoenix for negligence connected with the city's 911 emergency telephone response.[2]

## *"But Right Now... What Can I Do?"*

Chiquita Burt dialed 911 at 11:26 a.m. on a Saturday morning and reached the City of Phoenix emergency operator. Chiquita told the operator the whole story. Chiquita's ex-boyfriend, Craig Gardner, had been harassing her and threatening to damage her current boyfriend's car. Just the night before, Craig had tried to attack Chiquita in a night club, and threatened to kill her and her family. That same Friday night Chiquita had gone to the police to get a restraining order against Craig, but the police told her she would have to wait until the following Monday when the courts reopened.

---

[1] *See Bird v. State*, 821 P.2d 287 (Ariz. App. 1991) (interpreting provisions of the Actions Against Public Entities or Public Employees Act, Ariz. Rev. Stat. §§ 12-820 - 12-823); *City of Tucson v. Fahringer*, 795 P.2d 819 (Ariz. 1990) (legislative history of the Act); *compare Ryan v. State*, 656 P.2d 597 (Ariz. 1982) (rejecting common law governmental immunity).

[2] The facts and law of this case are set forth in *Hutcherson v. City of Phoenix*, 961 P.2d 449 (Ariz. 1998).

Through the night and into the morning hours, Craig had tried to find where Chiquita was staying. Chiquita took refuge in the apartment of her new boyfriend, professional football player Darryl Usher. Craig knew the location of Darryl's apartment, and called her at that apartment. Craig threatened to come over to "do something" to Darryl's car. Knowing of this threat, Darryl had said he would shoot Craig if he came over.

Chiquita asked the 911 operator what she could do to deal with Craig. The operator told her how to get a restraining order. Chiquita replied: *"But I'm talking about, about right now. What can I do?"*

The operator got the complete address and building description of Darryl's apartment from Chiquita. Twice during the conversation the operator told Chiquita an officer would be sent out. The operator also cautioned Chiquita that if Craig came to the house before the police arrived, Chiquita should call 911 again immediately.

Just 22 minutes after Chiquita hung up the phone, Craig crashed through Darryl's window and murdered both Chiquita and Darryl. Craig then shot himself in the head.

## *Low Emotion Means Slow Motion*

The mothers of the two victims sued the city for the negligent handling of the 911 call. Shocking facts were uncovered during the investigation. The 911 operator had placed a "Priority 3" on Chiquita's call—the *lowest* priority. The average police response time for Priority 3 calls was over 32 minutes. By comparison, calls for crimes in progress (Priority 1) had average 4.4 minutes response times, and domestic violence (Priority 2) calls had average 13.6 minute response times.

The operator made a lot of other mistakes. Because Chiquita had said Darryl might shoot Craig, the operator knew a firearm might be involved in a dispute. That fact alone should have elevated the priority. Chiquita had told the operator that Craig was on his way to Darryl's place, so the threat of violence was imminent. The operator later admitted she had downgraded the priority because Chiquita's tone of voice was calm and clear.

Also, in violation of departmental policy, the 911 operator had failed to send a special dispatch card to the police radio operators. This failure further slowed the response time, because the card would have told responding officers about the potential shooting about to occur.

Finally, the 911 operator had twice told Chiquita that officers were on the way. This statement likely caused Chiquita and Darryl to stay in the apartment rather than try to escape to a safer place. The operator had not told Chiquita that hers was being treated as a routine call and not a high priority call, and that the police would likely arrive in 30 minutes or more. The two victims had reasonably assumed the police were being dispatched immediately and would arrive in a matter of a few minutes.

Ironically, after the several gun shots were heard coming from Darryl's home, neighbors dialed 911... and the police did arrive in about 7 minutes.

A jury heard the case against the City, awarded the survivors of the two victims a total of $1.7 million, and held the City liable for 75% of that verdict (based on the jury's estimate of the City's "fault" for the deaths). The state Supreme Court let the verdict stand. "By creating a 911 system, [the city] accepted the obligation of attempting to prevent the very kind of harm that occurred here."

Ponder this idea: Chiquita had said that Darryl had a gun and would shoot Craig if Craig attacked. Did Darryl actually have a gun with ammunition, and the skill to use it? And if Darryl had a gun, why didn't he have it loaded and handy when Craig came in? Was it because Darryl had relied on the assurances of the 911 operator, and thought the gun wouldn't be necessary?

By providing 911 service, and by having "accepted the obligation of attempting to prevent" murderous attacks, does the city actually heighten the danger of citizens by telling them to "leave the crime fighting to us"?

A million dollar jury verdict does not answer the question.

# State of Arkansas

In Arkansas, "the doctrine of sovereign immunity is rigid."[1] The Arkansas state constitution expressly forbids a citizen from suing the state government in state courts.[2] (Under the 11th Amendment to the United States Constitution, citizens cannot sue states in federal courts.)

Officers and employees of the State of Arkansas are also immune from suit and from civil liability for damages arising from the negligent performance of their job duties.[3] There are two main exceptions. You can sue an employee who acts *maliciously* in the performance of his or her duty. You can sue an employee for negligence, but you can receive damages only to the extent of the employer's liability insurance.[4] Likewise, you can sue a city for negligence up to the limits of its insurance.[5]

---

[1]*Cross v. Arkansas Livestock and Poultry Commission*, 943 S.W.2d 230, 231 (Ark. 1997).

[2]Ark. Const. Art. 5 § 20.

[3]*Cross*, 943 S.W.2d at 233.

[4]*Id.* at 233.

[5]*City of Little Rock v. Weber*, 767 S.W.2d 529, 530-31 (Ark. 1989), *citing* Ark. Ann. Code of 1987 § 19-10-305 (Michie 1998).

If you dial 911 in Arkansas, and nobody responds, then you probably won't be able to sue the state for the police's failure to protect you or rescue you from criminal attack. You might be able to sue an officer or a city police department, but only if they carry liability insurance.

Your best defense against violent crime in Arkansas might be to rely on .357... not 911.

# State of California

California law takes a strong "no-duty" position on police liability for failure to protect citizens. Under a California statute, "[n]either a public entity nor a public employee is liable for failure to establish a police department or otherwise provide police protection service or... for failure to provide sufficient police protection service."[1] As one court wrote, "police officers have no affirmative statutory duty to do anything."[2]

California courts have consistently held that "the police owe no duty to crime victims in those cases where they have not acted to protect them."[3] The police can be held liable, however, if there is a "special relationship." A special relationship would exist: (1) if the police have made specific promises to take a particular action and failed to do so;[4] (2) if the police action created or increased the risk of harm to the victim;[5] or (3) if the police voluntarily started to aid an individual and by doing so lulled the individual into a false sense of security.[6]

---

[1]Cal. Govt. Code § 845, *quoted in Hartzler v. City of San Jose*, 120 Cal. Rptr. 5 (Cal. App. 1975).

[2]*Souza v. City of Antioch*, 62 Cal. Rptr. 2d 909, 916 (Cal. App, 1997). Note that the California Supreme Court ordered this case not to be officially published, and thus this case cannot be cited to any court as legal precedent.

[3]*Souza*, 62 Cal. Rptr. 2d at 916 (citing cases).

[4]*See Morgan v. County of Yuba*, 41 Cal. Rptr. 508 (Cal. App. 1964).

[5]*McCorkle v. City of Los Angeles*, 74 Cal. Rptr. 389, 449 P.2d 453 (Cal. 1969).

[6]*Mann v. State of California*, 139 Cal. Rptr. 82 (Cal. App. 1977).

The case of *Hartzler v. City of San Jose*[7], described below, shockingly illustrates how the law works in practice.

## *Please Call Back When Your Killer Arrives*

Over a period of a year, Ruth Bunnell had called the San Jose police at least 20 times to report that her estranged husband Mack had violently assaulted her and her two daughters. Mack had even been arrested once for an assault.

Mack called Ruth on September 4, 1972, and said he was coming to her house to kill her. Ruth called the police for immediate help. The police department "refused to come to her aid at that time, and asked that she call the department again when Mack Bunnell had arrived."[8]

Forty-five minutes later, Mack arrived and stabbed Ruth to death. Responding to a neighbor's call, the police came to Ruth's house... after she was dead.

Ruth's estate sued the city police for negligently failing to protect her. The police had known of Mack's violent past and Ruth's 20 previous calls. Yet when she called the police and told them of Mack's threat to kill her that day, the police outright refused to come.

The court held that the City of San Jose was shielded from the negligence suit because of the state statute, and because there was no "special relationship" between the police and Ruth. The police had not even

[7]*Hartzler v. City of San Jose*, 120 Cal. Rptr. 5 (Cal. App. 1975).

[8]*Hartzler*, 120 Cal. Rptr. at 6.

started to help her, and she had not relied on any promise that the police would help.

In every sense Ruth had no right to police protection. She dialed the equivalent of 911, and died.

# State of Colorado

The Colorado legislature enacted specials laws to assure that every "public entity shall be immune from liability in all claims" for personal injury or property damage with only a few exceptions.[1] Unlike many states, in Colorado it is possible to sue the police for failing to protect a citizen from harm.[2] Being able to sue does not automatically mean being able to win.[3] The general rule still applies: a police officer (or agency) owes no legal duty to prevent a person from harming other victims, unless there is a "special relationship" between the police and the criminal or between the police and the victims.[4]

How do the courts apply this rule in actual cases?

## *Out of Gas... Out of Luck*

Linda Whitcomb ran out of gas around midnight in a high crime area of Denver.[5] A nearby motel clerk wouldn't help her and even refused to give her change for her one and only five-dollar bill. Linda called 911

---

[1] Colorado Rev. Stat. § 24-10-106 (West Supp. 1998).

[2] *Leake v. Cain*, 720 P.2d 152 (Colo. 1986).

[3] Colorado law limits successful citizen damage claims against government entities to $150,000 per person injured, with a maximum payout of $600,000 for four or more persons involved in the same occurrence. Colorado Rev. Stat. § 114 (West Supp. 1998).

[4] *Potter v. Thieman*, 770 P.2d 1348, 1351 (Colo. App. 1989), *citing* Restatement (Second) of Torts § 315 (1965) and *Leake v. Cain*.

[5] The facts and law of this case are set forth in *Whitcomb v. City and County of Denver*, 731 P.2d 749 (Colo. App. 1986).

on a pay phone, and the police responded. The officers discovered that there was no "emergency" and that her car was not a traffic hazard. They refused to take her to a gas station, and had no idea where she might get a gas can. The officers offered to call a tow truck, but she didn't have enough money for that option. Unable or unwilling to do anything else to help, the officers left.

The early morning hours proved disastrous. Linda got a ride to a gas station from another couple, but was unable to get a gas can from the station or any of the patrons. Another woman at the gas station was having car trouble, and that woman vouched for two other men who could help Linda. The two other men agreed to take Linda back to her car with a container of gasoline. She got into their car. Instead of helping her, they assaulted her.

Linda sued the police for her damages. She argued that the police had a duty to provide her with adequate assistance to insure her safety. The case went to a jury which awarded her $18,750. The trial judge overturned that jury verdict. The Colorado Court of Appeals agreed with the trial judge.

No Colorado statute imposed any duty on the officers to protect Linda. In fact, the police enjoyed immunity to suits for negligently performing any "discretionary acts."[6] Before Linda could obtain damages from the police, she had to show that they done something to make her rely upon them for protection, such as promise to do something for her. Or, she had to show that the officers had made her situation even more dangerous than before they acted.

---

[6] *Id.* at 752.

In this case, the police had not done anything to cause Linda to rely on any promise or action. There "was no real emergency or hazard" facing Linda at the time they met with her.[7] And, according to the Court of Appeals, the police did nothing to make her situation any worse. Just calling 911 did not create any "special relationship" between the police and Linda.

Linda learned that a woman alone at midnight in a bad part of Denver cannot rely upon the police for protection. If she had known that she could not expect police help, would she have been wiser to travel armed?

## For Domestic Violence, Dialing 911 Is Not Enough

Jerome Perea broke into Yvonne Cossio's home on December 2, 1993, and assaulted her.[8] Her two children were in the home at the time. The 911 dispatcher recorded Yvonne's call under the category of "domestic violence" and specified that it involved a "boyfriend hitting caller," and that the boyfriend was an "unwanted party."

An officer responded at 10:30 a.m. to the Cossio residence. When the officer arrived the children were watching television, and he did not see what he considered evidence of domestic violence. Perea was there. Yvonne asked the officer to remove Perea from

---

[7]*Id.* at 751.

[8]The facts and law of this case are set forth in *Cossio v. City and County of Denver*, 986 F. Supp. 1340 (D. Colo. 1997)(federal court applying federal and Colorado law), *affirmed,* 139 F.3d 911 (10th Cir. 1998).

the house. The officer did not ask Yvonne if Perea had hit her, but escorted Perea out. The officer did run a check of Perea's police record and discovered that Perea was on probation for auto theft and was a gang member.

Denver Police Department policy required officers to "view all domestic violence complaints as instances of alleged criminal conduct." Officers were instructed that the "most appropriate law enforcement response" in cases of probable domestic violence is to arrest, charge, and take into custody any suspects involved.[9] The officer questioned no one, performed no other investigation, and did not arrest Perea.

About an hour after the officer left Yvonne's home, he was dispatched back there. He found Yvonne lying in the front yard of her home, shot to death by Perea.

Yvonne's heirs sued the police for negligently and recklessly mishandling the emergency call. The federal judge dismissed the lawsuit without a trial. The judge saw evidence of police negligence. The police officer should have conducted more investigation of the scene and the suspect. Negligence, however, is not enough to sue a city for damages. There wasn't enough evidence of reckless misconduct by the police. Case dismissed.

The police knew that a criminal and gang member had hit Yvonne, yet they were unable or unwilling to take steps necessary to protect her. The officer left her at the mercy of the suspect. By dialing 911, perhaps Yvonne had enraged Perea. When the police came and toothlessly left, Perea was free to take revenge...

---

[9] *Id.* at 1350.

because he knew that Yvonne was defenseless... and the police would do nothing until after the fact.

# State of Connecticut

Under the general rule in most states, an injured citizen cannot sue the police or the city government for their failure to protect the citizen from criminal attack. Under a Connecticut statute, if a police officer is held liable for failing to properly do his or her job, then the city may be liable to pay for the damages the officer caused to the victim.[1]

When can the police officer be held liable to the victim for negligently failing to protect? A crime victim can sue the officer only if the officer owed a "special duty" at that time to that specific identifiable individual, rather than merely to the public.[2] The officer would owe a "special duty" if the officer could see that his or her failure to act would likely put the specific identifiable person at risk of "imminent harm."[3]

When you call the police in an emergency, you are asking them to carry out their duties and enforce the law. What happens in Connecticut when the police officer fails to enforce the law?

## *Driver, Drunk & Weaving... No Duty*

Everyone knows that drunk drivers kill. For reckless or drunk driving, the convicted driver would face fines

---

[1] Conn. Gen. Stat. § 7-645, quoted in *Shore v. Town of Stonington*, 444 A.2d 1379, 1380 n.1 (Conn. 1982), (*reaffirmed by Sarno v. Whalen*, 659 A.2d 181 (Conn. 1995)).

[2] *Shore*, 444 A.2d at 1381-82; *Romano v. City of Derby*, 681 A.2d 387, 389 (Conn. App. 1996) (same rule).

[3] *Shore*, 444 A.2d at 1382; *Romano*, 681 A.2d at 389.

or prison time, or both.[4] As the law stood in 1980, police officers could lawfully stop a wayward driver and either warn him or remove him from the road. No Connecticut law required an officer to prevent drunk and reckless drivers from driving.[5]

When Sherry Shore was driving on the evening of January 14, 1980, she likely did not know that the police had no duty to protect her from known drunk and reckless drivers.[6] At 10:40 p.m. that evening, Officer Edward Sylvia, a Stonington police lieutenant, saw a speeding green Pontiac zip past him. Officer Sylvia turned his car around and followed the Pontiac. The officer saw the Pontiac swerve across the highway center line several times before it pulled into the parking lot of a social club.

Officer Sylvia parked in the same lot, spoke to the Pontiac's driver, Mark Cugini, and warned him to slow down and get someone to drive for him. There was enough evidence that Cugini was intoxicated when he spoke to Officer Sylvia, but the officer did not detain or arrest Cugini. Cugini went inside the club, and the officer drove away.

Less than an hour later, Cugini was behind the wheel of his speeding Pontiac when it crashed into Sherry Shore's car and killed her.

Could Ms. Shore's heirs sue the police officer and his department for negligently allowing Cugini to drive,

---

[4]Conn. Gen. Stat. § 14-222 (reckless driving) and § 14-227a (drunk driving), *quoted in Shore,* 444 A.2d 1379, 1380 nn.2-3.

[5]*Shore,* 444 A.2d at 1382-83.

[6]The facts and law of this case are set forth in *Shore v. Town of Stonington,* 444 A.2d 1379 (Conn. 1982).

when a reasonably alert and well-trained officer would have noticed Cugini was a drunk and reckless driver? The Connecticut Supreme Court said "no."

They could only sue the officer (and the city) if the officer owed a specific duty to protect Sherry Shore from Cugini. As the officer did not know Ms. Shore was in danger, he had no special duty to protect her. His only duty was to protect the "public" generally. The officer, the Court said, had no reason to know that Ms. Shore was in "imminent" danger from Cugini.

It's true that there were laws against reckless and drunk driving, but no Connecticut law required Officer Sylvia to enforce those laws by arresting all drunk drivers. The Court said, however, it would be wrong for officers to try to remove "from the road all persons who pose any potential hazard," because the officers might face liability for false arrest.

For failing to enforce the law, Connecticut cities and their police will usually not be held liable for damages in court.

## Bad Cop Kills... No Duty

A city is not "liable for damages to person or property" caused by the criminal conduct of its police officers.[7] Dawn Romano learned this legal lesson the hard way.[8]

Ms. Romano had been a friend of David Salemme, a police officer. Between March, 1988 and New Year's

---

[7] Conn. Gen. Stat. § 52-557n(a)(2)(A), *quoted in Romano v. City of Derby*, 681 A.2d at 390.

[8] The facts and law of this case are set forth in *Romano v. City of Derby*, 681 A.2d 387 (Conn. App. 1996).

Eve that year, Ms. Romano had reported to police that Officer Salemme had engaged in heated arguments with her and had physically abused her. Late in December, 1988, Ms. Romano told police that Salemme had threatened to hurt her again, and that she feared more violence against her. The police officers who received the later reports, and knew about the history of the two individuals, did not think that Ms. Romano was in danger.

On New Year's Eve, Officer Salemme shot Ms. Romano several times before he killed himself. Ms. Romano survived and sued the city for the police officers' negligently failing to protect her. The appellate court of Connecticut agreed with the trial court: Ms. Romano didn't have a case.

The court noted that, when Ms. Romano reported Salemme's last threats, she did not describe her earlier problems with Salemme. Also, she did not try to get a protective order against Salemme, and the police officers did not witness Salemme physically hurting Ms. Romano. These facts showed that the police did not know that Ms. Romano was facing a risk of "imminent harm" from Salemme, and therefore they (actually the city) could not be sued for failing to protect her. Moreover, the city was not liable for Salemme's criminal acts anyway.

Nearly eight years after she called the police to protect her from a violent fellow police officer, Ms. Romano learned from the appellate court that she could not even sue for damages. It's just too bad that Ms. Romano had not been properly armed to defend herself against Salemme, the bad cop who the police wouldn't stop.

# State of Delaware

The Delaware state legislature has declared that the state government and its employees cannot be sued, so long as they are performing official duties in good faith, are exercising discretionary powers, and are not acting with gross negligence.[1] All other governmental entities, such as counties and cities, and their employees, are also immune from most tort lawsuits seeking damages for the government's failure to carry out its legal duties.[2] Even in those few cases where a citizen can sue the government for damages, there is a $300,000 limit on how much the courts can award (unless the government entity is insured for a larger amount).[3]

In one case where a riot took place, the Supreme Court of Delaware held that a store owner could not sue the City of Wilmington for failing to provide adequate and timely fire protection.[4] The Fire Chief had ordered that the fire equipment *not* be sent to the riot area until a report of fire was confirmed and the police agreed to escort the firefighters to the scene. The store owner's business was set ablaze and was virtually destroyed before firefighters ever came.

The Court said that a Delaware city government does not have a duty "to protect private property from

---

[1] Del. Code Ann. tit. 10, § 4001 (Michie Supp. 1998).

[2] Del. Code Ann. tit. 10, § 4011. Exceptions are set forth in tit. 10, § 4012.

[3] Del. Code Ann. tit. 10, § 4013(a).

[4] The facts and law of this case are set forth in *Biloon's Electrical Service, Inc. v. City of Wilmington*, 417 A.2d 371 (Del. 1980), *affirming* 401 A.2d 636 (Del. Super. 1979).

riotous conduct." Therefore, a citizen cannot sue the city for failing to keep the peace.

# District of Columbia

Washington, District of Columbia (D.C.) is home to the three branches of the national government, several military bases, the Federal Bureau of Investigation, and most of the federal regulatory agencies. Federal Park Police patrol the federal properties. The District also has a local government with courts and a police force. Despite all of this police and military power amassed in just 10 square miles, if you have an emergency and call 911... *you are on your own.*

## Burglary, Assault, Rape: "Investigate the Trouble"

Carolyn, Joan and Miriam were asleep in their rooms during the early morning hours of March 16, 1975, when the attack began. Their slumber was shattered when two men broke down the back door of the three floor house in Northwest Washington. The men first entered the second floor room of Miriam and her four year old daughter, and violently sexually assaulted Miriam there.

From the third floor room they shared, Carolyn and Joan heard Miriam's screams from below. Carolyn called the police and told the duty officer that the house was being burglarized and that they needed immediate assistance. The call had come in at 6:23 a.m. Three minutes later the call was radioed to the street officers as a "Code 2," which was a lower priority than the "Code 1" given to crimes in progress.

Four police cruisers responded to the dispatch, and three went to the women's address. Meanwhile,

Carolyn and Joan crawled out their window onto a neighboring rooftop to wait for the police. One of the police cars drove through the alley without stopping to check the back door, and then went around to the front of the house. A second police officer knocked on the front door, but left when he got no answer. All three officers left the scene at 6:33 a.m., just five minutes after they had arrived.

The two women crawled back into their room, still heard Miriam's screams, and called the police again. The duty officer assured them that help was on the way, but the call was logged at 6:42 a.m. as "investigate the trouble" and never dispatched to any officers.

Shortly later the two women thought the police were in the home and called out to them. There were no policemen there, but the attackers heard the shouts and came upstairs. All three women were kidnapped, taken to one of the attacker's homes and raped, robbed, beaten, and sexually abused—for 14 hours.

The three women victims sued the District of Columbia and the officers for negligently failing to provide adequate police protection. *Their complaint was dismissed before a jury ever heard the evidence.* Under D.C. law, "official police personnel and the government employing them are not generally liable to victims of criminal acts for failure to proved adequate police protection."[1] According to the courts, this rule "rests upon the fundamental principle that a government and its agents are under no general duty

---

[1] *Warren v. District of Columbia*, 444 A.2d 1, 4 (D.C. 1981) (*en banc*) (quoting the trial court decision).

to provide public services, such as police protection, to any particular individual citizen."[2]

## *Feel Safe in the Nation's Capital?*

The general no-duty rule remains the law in the District. Unless there is a "special relationship" between the citizen and the police officer or department,[3] the police owe no legal duty to protect specific individuals from danger[4], even foreseeable criminal violence.[5]

Meanwhile, the District of Columbia practically prohibits the private possession of firearms.[6] The violent crime rate there is among the highest in the nation.[7]

Enjoy your next visit to the Capital... if you can.

---

[2] *Id.*

[3] See the discussion of "special relationship" in the chapter entitled "Brief Summary of the Law."

[4] *Wanzer v. District of Columbia*, 580 A.2d 127 (D.C. 1990) (emergency call to 911 does not create a "special relationship" between the caller and the ambulance service; therefore the ambulance service owes no legal duty to the caller, and cannot be liable for failing to respond to the call).

[5] *Morgan v. District of Columbia*, 468 A.2d 1306 (D.C. 1983)(*en banc*).

[6] D.C. Code § 6-2312 prohibits registration of any pistol not registered before September 24, 1976 (does not apply to retired Metropolitan Police officers). D.C. Code § 22-3204 makes it a felony to possess any unlicensed firearm of any kind, or to possess any (pre-1976 registered) firearm whatsoever when not on one's own property or business.

[7] See Federal Bureau of Investigation, *Crime in the United States* 77 (1998).

# State of Florida

Do the police in Florida owe you a legal duty to protect you from criminal attack? In that state, the police officer's duty is to protect "the citizens" or "the public as a whole."[1] The victim of a criminal offense cannot sue the police for failing to take "reasonable law enforcement action" which would have prevented the crime, unless the police owe a "special duty" to that individual.[2]

A few brief examples show how Florida law has been operating.

## *Miami Was Hot, Hot, Hot*

Fearing disorder surrounding the Republican National Convention in August, 1968, local merchants asked Miami and Dade County police forces to provide protection.[3] Police were stationed in the area on August 7 while demonstrations took place outside the Convention. By order of the mayor and sheriff, the police were removed from the area later that night. After the police left, the demonstrations soon erupted into mob violence. Rioters plundered the local merchants' stores and caused considerable damage.

Could the merchants sue the city and its police? The Supreme Court of Florida said "no." The "authorities ought to be left free to exercise their discretion and choose the tactics deemed appropriate without worry

---

[1]*Everton v. Willard*, 468 So. 2d 936, 938 (Fla. 1985).

[2]*Id.*

[3]The facts and law of this case are set forth in *Wong v. City of Miami*, 237 So. 2d 132 (Fla. 1970).

over possible allegations of negligence," the Court said. Indeed, "inherent in the right to exercise police powers is the right to determine strategy and tactics for the deployment of those powers."[4] The police knew of the risk of harm, had initially provided police protection, and the merchants had doubtless relied on that protection. *Those facts didn't matter*. The police would not be liable for failing to protect citizens from violent crime.

## Paperwork Lost...
## Prosecutor Immune

Diana McFarland had repeatedly gone to the Jacksonville Police for help in dealing with her former boyfriend's threats and abuse.[5] The police didn't stop the boyfriend's conduct, but on one occasion the police advised Diana to ask the State Attorney to help her get a restraining order. She contacted the State Attorney's office, and was assured that actions would be taken to help her, including getting a restraining order (known as an "injunction for protection").

The paperwork was misplaced or misfiled. The State Attorney's office did nothing. Diana's boyfriend continued to abuse her and she kept asking the police for help. Diana was not protected and the boyfriend did not stop until he had murdered Diana.

---

[4]*Id.* at 134.

[5]The facts and law of this case are set forth in *Office of the State Attorney v. Parrotino*, 628 So. 2d 1097 (Fla. 1993).

Could Diana's heirs sue the police department or the State Attorney's office for negligently failing to protect her? "No" on all counts, said the Florida courts.[6]

In particular, the Florida Supreme Court stated that a citizen cannot sue a state prosecutor, because the prosecutor is immune. "Both judges and prosecutors alike should be free from the threat of suit for their official actions, because permitting suit in this situation could deter a full and unfettered exercise of judicial or quasi-judicial authority."[7]

Predicting the outcome of government negligence cases under Florida law is not easy. The state and local governments can be sued for negligence in some cases, but deciding whether the government will be liable in a particular case is a complicated process.[8] Even if the citizen wins a negligence suit, there may be a cap on the damage award.[9] The Florida Supreme Court has made clear, however, that state prosecutors cannot be sued by citizens who are injured by the prosecutor's decisions about law enforcement.[10] The same kind of immunity that protects a prosecutor also protects a police officer's decisions about whether to arrest a suspect.[11]

---

[6]*Id.* at 1098.

[7]*Id.* at 1098-99.

[8]*See Commercial Carrier Corp. v. Indian River County*, 371 So. 2d 1010, 1018-1021 (Fla. 1979) (interpreting Fla. Stat. § 768.28 (waiver of immunity)).

[9]Fla. Stat. Ann. § 768.28(5), *quoted in Commercial Carrier*, 371 So. 2d at 1014.

[10]*Parrotino*, 628 So. 2d at 1098-99.

[11]*Everton*, 468 So. 2d at 939. *See also Bowden v. Henderson*, 700 So. 2d 714, 717 (Fla. App. 1997) (following *Everton*, police

If you fear a criminal attack in Florida, remember that the police may not owe you a duty to protect you. Wondering whether your heirs can sue the police after you are dead might be an interesting legal question... but a cold comfort in the Sunshine State.

---

owe no duty to specific individuals unless there is a special relationship), *review granted*, 717 So. 2d 532 (Fla. 1998).

# State of Georgia

The Georgia Supreme Court made it clear in 1993: the police owe a duty to protect the public in general, but in most cases they owe no duty to protect "any particular member of the public."[1] This rule, called the "public duty" doctrine, does not apply when there is a "special relationship" between the individual citizen and the city or county government.[2]

The "special relationship" can arise when:

(1) the police, by their promises or actions, give an "explicit assurance" to "act on behalf" of the victim;

(2) the police know that their failure to act could result in harm coming to the victim; and

(3) the victim justifiably relied on the police's action and was harmed because he or she relied on the police but the police failed to act properly.[3]

If the crime victim has evidence to prove all of these three factors, then the victim can sue the police and at least get a trial. The trial jury would then decide whether the police acted negligently under the circumstances, and whether the police or city government should pay damages.

The Georgia Supreme Court's decision in *City of Rome v. Jordan*[4] shows just how narrowly that state's

---

[1] *City of Rome v. Jordan*, 426 S.E.2d 861, 862-63 (Ga. 1993).

[2] *Id.* at 863.

[3] *Id.*

[4] The facts and law of this case are set forth in *City of Rome v. Jordan*, 426 S.E.2d 861 (Ga. 1993). The Court affirmed summary

courts will treat the "special relationship" exception to the rule.

## *Police Too Busy—No Duty*

Hoyt Marks escaped from an alcohol rehabilitation center and appeared early one morning at the home of Patricia and Cary Jordan. Marks demanded to see his estranged wife Dana. Before letting Marks in, Patricia telephoned Dana at her mother's house nearby. Dana told Patricia to let Marks in, and Dana would call the police.

Patricia, who was alone in the house, let Marks inside. Meanwhile, Dana called the police and told them that Marks was loose, that there was an outstanding warrant for his arrest for probation violation, and that he was harassing Patricia. The police dispatcher told Dana that a police car was on its way.

There was no police car on its way. Because of a shooting incident elsewhere, no police units were available.[5]

Marks attacked Patricia and sexually assaulted her at knifepoint. Dana called the house again. With a knife at her throat, Patricia was allowed to answer the call. Dana asked her if the police had arrived yet, and Patricia said "no". Dana told Patricia that she would call the police again. After she hung up, Marks assaulted Patricia again. The police never came in time to prevent the repeated assaults and injuries.

---

judgment against Patricia Jordan; she never even got a trial.

[5]*Id.* at 866 (concurring opinion by Justice Hunstein).

Could Patricia sue the police department for saying they would come but failing to protect her? The police owed her no duty to protect her from the criminal attacks unless she could prove a "special relationship."

Patricia testified that she did not try to fight Marks' attacks because she thought the police were coming. The state Supreme Court held, however, that Patricia did not know whether the police had promised to help her, and she could not rely on any such police promise. As the Court wrote: "Any reliance on her part on the police arriving was based solely on a belief that the police would come if called, not on any promise made by the police."[6]

When in Georgia, take note: your naive "belief that the police would come if called" is legally worthless. Either plan to protect yourself against criminal attack, or pray that the police are not too busy to respond to your 911 emergency call.

---

[6]*Id.* at 864.

# State of Hawaii

Do the police in America's 50th state owe a legal duty to protect citizens against criminal attack? The Supreme Court of Hawaii has adopted the "generally accepted proposition" that "the failure of the police to provide protection is ordinarily not actionable."[1] In other words, in most cases crime victims cannot sue the police for failing to protect them from criminal attack.

Hawaiian law recognizes an exception to this no-duty rule. If the action of the police *increased* the victim's risk of harm, and the police negligently failed to protect the victim against that increased risk, then the police can be held liable for the victim's resulting damages.[2] As described below, the exception works to protect the police from liability... not to protect people from violent crime.

## *Police Didn't Make Things Any Worse*

Brotherly love was apparently lost on the Freitas family.[3] Jerry Freitas had a record of convictions for violent crimes, a history of mental instability, and a reputation for violence. On November 24, 1973, Jerry drove the short distance to his brother John's house, firing his rifle out the window as he was driving. Upon

---

[1]*Freitas v. City and County of Honolulu*, 574 P.2d 529, 532 (Haw. 1978), citing Riss v. City of New York, 240 N.E.2d 860 (N.Y. 1968).

[2]*Freitas*, 574 P.2d at 532, *citing Schuster v. City of New York*, 154 N.E.2d 534 (N.Y. 1958).

[3]The facts and law of this case are set forth in *Freitas v. City and County of Honolulu*, 574 P.2d 529 (Haw. 1978).

arrival at the house, Jerry threatened and terrorized the people there. Another brother, Raynard Freitas, learned of this attack (presumably by telephone) and rushed over to John's house.

When Raynard arrived, Jerry left. The Honolulu police were contacted and two officers responded to the scene. The three Freitas brothers told the police that their (fourth) brother Jerry had pointed a loaded rifle at and threatened to kill them, and had also terrorized the neighborhood. Other non-family witnesses confirmed these facts to the police. The brothers told the police also about Jerry's history of criminal behavior and mental disturbance. One of the officers knew of previous conflicts between Jerry and John. Raynard also told the officers that Jerry had a fully automatic machine gun and police-style revolver.

The Honolulu police officers only minimally investigated the case and did not arrest Jerry for attacking and terrorizing his brothers and others. About six weeks later, Jerry shot his three brothers and permanently injured them.

The Supreme Court of Hawaii held that the three brothers could not sue the police department or the individual officers for negligence, because the police owed no duty to protect the brothers from Jerry's violence. According to the Court, there was no evidence that the police did anything to *worsen* the brothers' situation or to increase their risk of harm from Jerry. Without such evidence, the brothers' case had to be dismissed without a trial.

The "gun control" laws of Hawaii severely hamper a citizen's ability to protect himself or herself from criminal attack.[4] Yet Hawaiian police might decide not to arrest your attacker. They might choose to ignore your 911 call.

Hawaii is a particularly beautiful place. Too bad its government moves to disarm the people but refuses to take responsibility for protecting them. Has *"aloha"* come to mean *"welcome—but watch your back"*?

---

[4]Haw. Rev. Stat. §§ 134-1 - 134-18.

# State of Idaho

Can a citizen sue the state of Idaho, one of its cities, or a local police department, for failing to protect him from criminal attack? The law in Idaho is uncertain on this question, but it appears that the answer is: "Yes, the citizen can sue. That doesn't mean the citizen will win."

Two Idaho statutes make suing the state or the police unattractive. First, the state and city governments can not be held liable for damages caused by their failing to prevent or suppress mob violence, riots, or other civil disturbances.[1] Second, the law limits the maximum amount an injured citizen can recover in damages from the government; the maximum damage award is $500,000, unless insurance coverage exists for more.[2]

## *Busted Nose, Wobbly On His Feet... Let Him Drive*

A bouncer in a local bar had punched Barton Webster in the nose.[3] In the early morning hours of June 22, 1986, just after the assault, Webster drove to the police station to file a criminal complaint against the bouncer. Police officers told Webster to get medical attention first, then file the complaint. One officer suspected Webster had been drinking and advised him to ride an ambulance instead of drive to the hospital.

---

[1]Idaho Code § 6-904(b) (Michie 1998).

[2]Idaho Code § 6-926.

[3]The facts and law of this case are set forth in *Olguin v. City of Burley*, 810 P.2d 255 (Idaho 1991).

Webster refused that advice and drove to the hospital alone. The doctor who treated Webster saw he was too drunk to drive and called the police. The same police officers came to the hospital. The officers told Webster to call someone to pick him up, but not to drive himself. Then the officers gave Webster his keys and left.

Shortly after the officers left, Webster drove his car away. Less than an hour later, Webster crashed into another driver's car and seriously injured the passenger. The passenger's mother and guardian sued the City and the two police officers for releasing Webster to drive when they had good reason to believe he was too drunk to drive.

The trial court dismissed the lawsuit before trial. Five years after the accident, the Idaho Supreme Court held that the trial court was correct. The police had the legal power to arrest Webster for a violation of law committed in their presence,[4] or for violating any law.[5] One statute even made it the "duty of peace officers within the State of Idaho to enforce and make arrests for the violation of" certain misdemeanor motor vehicle laws.[6]

Yet as there was no statute that required the police to prevent Webster from driving drunk by keeping his car keys, they had no legal duty to do so. Without a duty, the police could not be held liable for damages. Case closed.

---

[4]Idaho Code § 19-603(1).

[5]Idaho Code § 50-209.

[6]Idaho Code § 49-205(3).

Do the police in Idaho owe a duty to protect you there? You might never really know until you dial 911...

# State of Illinois

Under Illinois law, city and county governments are generally not liable for failing to supply police protection.[1] Similarly, the governments are not legally liable for the injuries that police officers negligently cause while performing their official duties.[2] A "special duty" exception to the rule exists which, if proved, would allow a victim of police negligence to sue. To invoke the exception, the victim must prove all four of the following elements:

(1) the police (government) was "uniquely aware" of the danger to the victim;

(2) the police did or failed to do some specific act;

(3) the act (or failure to act) was "affirmative or willful in nature;" and

(4) the victim was injured while he or she was under the direct and immediate control of the police (government's employees).[3]

Can the city police be liable for failing to respond to a crime victim who dials 911?

## *Sit and Watch for the Police*

Sylvia Galuszynski and her mother heard noises in the evening of January 24, 1984, and discovered an intruder trying to break into their Chicago home.[4] At

---

[1]*Leone v. City of Chicago*, 619 N.E.2d 119, 121 (Ill. 1993); 745 Ill. Comp. Stat. 10/1-101, 10/4-102 (West 1992).

[2]*Leone*, 619 N.E.2d at 122.

[3]*Id.*

[4]The facts and law of this case are set forth in *Galuszynski v.*

9:45 p.m., Sylvia dialed 911 to report the imminent invasion. The 911 operator, a police department employee, answered the call, took the information, and told Sylvia to "watch for the police" because they were on the way.

The police were not on their way; they did not arrive until 10:10 p.m. By then, the armed invaders had attacked and injured Sylvia and her mother, and had stolen money, jewelry and other items. Could Sylvia and her mother sue the police for failing to promptly respond to the emergency 911 call?

The Illinois court recited the statutory law: "Neither a local public entity nor a public employee is liable... for failure to provide adequate police protection or service, [for] failure to prevent the commission of crimes, [or for] failure to apprehend criminals."[5] The Court went on to say that "the duty of the police is to preserve the well-being of the community at large." That duty "is generally not owed to specific individuals."

Sylvia and her mother would lose their case under the general rule. But what about the "special duty" exception (set forth above)?

The court held that Sylvia and her mother had offered evidence for the first three elements of the "special duty" exception. Then came the bad news: they had no evidence or proof of the fourth element. The two victims could not show that they had been

---

*City of Chicago,* 475 N.E.2d 960 (Ill. App. 1985).

[5]*Galuszynski,* 475 N.E.2d at 961, *quoting* the Local Government and Governmental Employees Tort Immunity Act , §4-102, now codified at 745 Ill. Comp. Stat. 10/4-102.

under the "direct and immediate control" of the police when they suffered their injuries. The police had not placed the two women into danger by anything the police had done. Therefore, the Court held, the police had owed no legal duty to respond to protect the women from the ongoing attack.

## *Ditched, Battered and Bewildered*

Even when the police are on site they have little duty to protect citizens. Valiant Poliny and Donald Nagolski were walking in Chicago on July 20, 1985, when Rolando Calderon attacked and beat them.[6] Witnesses took Nagolski to the hospital, while Poliny followed Calderon up the street. Soon Poliny flagged a police car and led the two officers to Calderon.

Calderon was standing with some friends, one of whom was Jose Rosario. While the officers were arresting Calderon, Rosario and another man verbally abused Poliny and threatened to hurt him because he had helped the police arrest Calderon. Poliny asked the officers to help him get to the station house to file his complaint. He also asked the officers specifically not to leave him alone with Rosario. The officers refused Poliny's requests and left the scene. Rosario attacked and battered Poliny after the police were gone.

Poliny sued the officers and the police department for negligently failing to protect him from Rosario. The appellate court of Illinois upheld the trial court ruling: Poliny's case was dismissed.

---

[6]The facts and law of this case are set forth in *Poliny v. Soto*, 533 N.E.2d 15 (Ill. App. 1998).

Under the general rule, the Chicago police owed no duty to protect Poliny. The "special duty" exception also did not apply, because Poliny "was not in the immediate control of the police when he was attacked by Rosario."[7] The fact that the police knew of the threats against Poliny but just left him alone on the street to face the hoodlums, did not move the court even to allow a trial against the police.

Fortunately, Sylvia Galuszynski and Valiant Poliny survived the attacks on them... no thanks to the 911 operators or to the police. Would the attacks have taken place if the intended victims had been equipped and ready to defend themselves with firearms?

---

[7]*Id.* at 18.

# State of Indiana

Indiana's legislature has declared that governmental entities and their employees cannot be held liable for negligence in the "performance of a discretionary function."[1] The government also cannot be held liable for negligently failing to enforce the law.[2]

Police cannot be sued for negligence when they so poorly investigate a rape case that the rapist goes unapprehended until he kills another victim.[3] That result comes from the rule that the police owe their duties to the public as a whole, but not to any particular individual.

To sue a city for negligence, the victim must prove that the city owed a duty, not just to the public, but to that particular person. Such a special legal duty only exists when (1) the city has explicitly assured the person that the city would act on the person's behalf, (2) the city knew that failing to act could lead to harm to the person, and (3) the person could justifiably rely on the city's assurances and actions on the person's behalf.[4]

Even where the government can be sued, there are limits on governmental liability of $300,000 per person, with a maximum of $5,000,000 for any given incident.[5]

---

[1]Ind. Code. Ann. § 34-13-3-3(6); § 34-4-16.5-3(6).

[2]Ind. Code. Ann. § 34-13-3-3(7).

[3]*Crouch v. Hall*, 406 N.E.2d 303, 304-05 (Ind. App. 1980)

[4]*Mullin v. Municipal City of South Bend*, 639 N.E.2d 278, 284 (Ind. 1994).

[5]Ind. Code. Ann. § 34-13-3-4.

Indiana law declares that the police have a duty to preserve the peace, prevent violations of law, detect and arrest criminals, suppress riots, and protect the rights of persons and property.[6] Even so, the Indiana courts have held that when a police force fails to carry out those duties, and a crime wave destroys a business, the injured citizen cannot sue.[7] How does the law apply when lives are at stake, and someone dials 911?

## *Hang Up on the Tenth Ring... You're Dead*

David Lewis, 52, suffered a heart attack at about 5:30 p.m. on October 26, 1987.[8] His adult stepdaughter Vanessa Riggs dialed 911 three separate times. She let the phone ring at least 10 times, but there was no answer. Vanessa called her grandmother, who dialed 911, got an answer, and reported the emergency.

As the 10 minutes passed, David stopped breathing. Paramedics eventually arrived and restarted his heart, but he had suffered brain and heart damage from the lack of oxygen. About four months later, David died, in large part because of the heart damage.

Mrs. Lewis sued the city police department for negligently failing to timely answer the 911 calls. The city's 911 system channeled all 911 calls through the

---

[6]Ind. Code. Ann. § 36-8-3-10(a), formerly Indiana Code § 18-1-11-7.

[7]*Simpson's Food Fair, Inc. v. City of Evansville*, 272 N.E.2d 871, 872-73 (Ind. App. 1971).

[8]The facts and law of this case are set forth in *Lewis v. City of Indianapolis*, 554 N.E.2d 13 (Ind. App. 1990).

same switchboard that handled emergency calls, administrative business calls, and personal calls. Emergency calls therefore had to wait until operators finished existing non-emergency calls. Once the operator received a medical emergency call, the operator would connect the call directly to the major hospital center. The switchboard system was a bottleneck that could, and did, delay emergency calls.

Mrs. Lewis's case never went to a jury, because the trial court dismissed it on a motion. The state court of appeal upheld the ruling: "The City and Department owed a duty to the public in the discharge of their 911 responsibilities." The police owed the duty to the public at large, but not to any specific individual, unless there existed a "special duty." The police 911 system owed no "special duty" to David Lewis because the police and city did not know that he was in danger and had never promised to help him personally.

When the 911 system fails, the citizen is on his own.[9]

---

[9]Indiana Code section 34-4-16.5-3(17) was enacted in 1988 to immunize governments from liability for nearly every aspect of liability arising from their 911 "enhanced emergency telephone system." *Lewis*, 554 N.E.2d at 16 n. 3.

# State of Iowa

Concerning the duty of cities and their police to protect individual citizens, Iowa follows the same general rules of many other states. State laws allow citizens to sue the state[1] or the city government[2] for negligence, but other laws prevent law suits which claim that the government was negligent in carrying out a "discretionary function."[3] In addition, citizens cannot sue the government for negligently performing (or failing to perform) a "public duty."[4]

Providing police service is a public duty. That rule means the police owe no duty to protect any particular individual... and bad police judgment results in death.

## *Police Foul Up, A Child Dies... No Duty*

Just after midnight on April 11, 1987, two men banged on the door of Donald and Janet Allen's mobilehome near Ottumwa, Iowa.[5] The Allens awoke, and the two men asked to test drive the pickup truck which the Allens had advertised for sale. Janet agreed to take the two men for the drive.

During the drive, the two men pulled a knife on Janet and tied her up with duct tape. When they returned to the mobilehome, the two men tied up

---

[1] Iowa Code Ann. § 669.4.

[2] Iowa Code Ann. § 670.2.

[3] Iowa Code Ann. § 669. 14(1) (state), § 670.4(3) (cities).

[4] *Hildenbrand v. Cox*, 369 N.W.2d 411, 415 (Iowa 1985).

[5] The facts and law of this case are set forth in *Allen v. Anderson*, 490 N.W.2d 848 (Iowa App. 1992).

Donald. Then the men raped the Allens' 16-year-old daughter, and then duct taped their 12-year-old daughter. Both girls were loaded into the rapists' station wagon.

The parents resisted being put into the car. Donald broke free and ran to a neighbor's house for help. Meanwhile, the 16-year-old struggled without success to free the 12-year-old and get her out of the pickup. Janet was held at knife point while she fought one of the men, and stopped only when her throat was cut. The 16-year-old escaped to another neighbor's home.

After hearing Donald's story, the neighbor called 911 at 12:44 a.m. At the same time, Donald saw the two men leave with the 12-year-old girl in the station wagon. Within one minute of receiving the radio dispatch, one Ottumwa police officer positioned himself at a key intersection to intercept the station wagon. He chased one suspected car for a minute, but decided it was the wrong one, and returned to his outlook post. He stayed their 20 minutes.

Meanwhile, two sheriff's deputies arrived at the Allens' residence at 12:56 a.m. The deputies learned of the kidnapping, and one deputy called the dispatcher. The dispatcher put him on hold three times during the conversation: once to dispatch an ambulance, and twice to dispatch officers to check on an illegally parked car in town. Officer Chiles was already in the field and responded to the parking violation.

The deputies learned that the two men were headed for a particular residence in Ottumwa,[6] and the

---

[6]The case report does not indicate how the deputies learned this fact.

dispatcher agreed to send police to that destination which was only three minutes from the police station. The deputies relied on the dispatcher to follow through, so the deputies did not travel to that destination themselves. At that moment, two other officers were within one minute of the kidnappers' destination.

The dispatcher, however, failed to issue an all-points bulletin for the two criminals. Instead, the dispatcher took a call about harassing phone calls and then wrote a note about the Allens' situation to the shift supervisor, Officer Anderson, who was in the office. After reading the note, Officer Anderson decided that he wanted Officer Chiles to report back to the police station. The dispatcher radioed Officer Chiles, who was investigating the illegally parked car, to report to base. The dispatcher failed to tell Officer Chiles that the call was an emergency.

Fifteen minutes later, Officer Anderson wondered where Officer Chiles was, and then left the station looking for him. Officer Chiles was found still working the illegally parked car case.

Officer Anderson then ordered all but one of the available officers on duty to report to a parking lot for a briefing. Six officers assembled and received information about the crime, but they were not told about the kidnapping. All six drove to the criminals' expected destination and arrived at 1:32 a.m., but by then the criminals were long gone. The woman there said the two men had come, had switched cars, and had driven off with an unidentified female in the car. They had left between 10 and 20 minutes before the officers arrived.

The kidnappers attempted to rape the 12-year old girl and then murdered her later that morning.

The Allens sued the city and the police for failing to adequately respond to the 911 call and protect their young daughter. The trial court dismissed their lawsuit without a trial. On review, the Iowa appeals court stated that the duty of the police "to protect the citizenry is owed to the public and not to individuals."

It didn't matter to the court that, for example, the shift supervisor Officer Anderson was hired for an administrative position, had no supervisor training and no training on hostage or kidnapping situations, but did have continuing physical and psychological problems due to a previous head injury. It didn't matter that it was a misdemeanor crime to fail to respond when an officer requests assistance to make an arrest or prevent a crime.[7] It didn't matter that the sheriff's deputies had relied on the dispatcher to send officers immediately to the criminals' destination, and thus did not themselves try to free the young girl.

No duty to provide police protection means that the police are not held responsible for glaring errors and incompetence that result in innocent deaths. Can you depend upon Iowa police to protect you? How about when they promise they will? Consider the following case.

## *Your Call Can Wait Till Monday*

Harvey Spencer, on April 18, 1989, threatened to kill his former girlfriend Victoria Graham.[8] The next

---

[7]Iowa Code Ann. § 719.2.

[8]The facts and law of this case are set forth in *Hawkeye Bank &*

day, Officer Williams investigated the threat and concluded that Harvey would indeed try to kill Victoria. The officer advised her to stay somewhere else temporarily, but she refused. The officer then told her that an extra police watch would be placed on her and her home, and that officers would try to find Harvey and would watch for him in her neighborhood.

Two days later, on April 20, Officer Dippold was the first officer to actually do any of the things Officer Williams had promised. Officer Dippold looked for Harvey but did not find him, and then decided that the matter could wait until Monday, April 22.

No other police took any other action to protect Victoria. Nobody told Victoria that the promised extra protection would not come. At 2:00 a.m. on April 23, Harvey invaded Victoria's home. Victoria called 911 and was told that help was on the way. That "help" was too late. Harvey killed her and another man that morning.

The estates of the two dead victims sued the police and the city for failing to provide the promised extra protection. No jury ever heard the case, however, because the trial court dismissed it on a motion filed by the city's lawyer.

On appeal, the Iowa court refused to hold the police and the city liable for promising protection and then not providing it. The police can be liable for their negligence only when "the police create the situation which places the citizen's life in jeopardy" or when "the police take a citizen into custody." Neither of these exceptions to the rule applied here.

---

*Trust Co. v. Spencer*, 487 N.W.2d 94 (Iowa App. 1992).

Victoria had relied on the extra police protection, and thus had not tried to get additional protection through the court system or by hiring a private guard. She apparently did not arm herself for protection. When the expected attack came, Victoria was undefended. She dialed 911... and died.

# State of Kansas

Like many states, Kansas has a Tort Claims Act which regulates whether citizens can sue the state and local governments. That Act holds governmental entities liable for their negligent acts, with certain important exceptions.[1] Citizens cannot sue the government for negligently enforcing or failing to enforce the law,[2] for negligently performing or failing to perform a discretionary function,[3] or for failing to provide police or fire protection.[4] In fact, citizens cannot sue the government for adopting and enforcing, or failing to adopt or enforce, written personnel policies designed to protect persons' health and safety.[5]

The Kansas Supreme Court has expressly held that, under the common law, "the duty of a law enforcement officer to preserve the peace is a duty owed to the public at large." Unless there is "some special relationship with or specific duty owed [to] an individual," the city cannot be held liable for failing to protect an individual.[6] The Kansas statutes did not change that no-duty rule.

---

[1] Kan. Stat. Ann. § 75-6103.

[2] Kan. Stat. Ann. § 75-6104(c).

[3] Kan. Stat. Ann. § 75-6104(e).

[4] Kan. Stat. Ann. § 75-6104(h).

[5] Kan. Stat. Ann. § 75-6104(d).

[6] *Woodruff v. City of Ottawa*, 951 P.2d 953, 954, 958 (Kan. 1997)(court's syllabus; citation omitted).

## Police Order Citizen Off His Own Property—Trespasser Burns It

Kansas courts have enforced that no-duty rule in several cases. For example, in one case a citizen called the police to have a drunk trespasser removed from his property.[7] When the police arrived, the citizen warned that the trespasser would try to burn his house down. The officers told the *citizen* to leave, but left the trespasser on the property. Sure enough, fifteen minutes later the citizen's house burned. The Kansas Supreme Court held that the officers' decision was a "discretionary function," and the police owed a legal duty to protect the general public and but not individual citizens. The police owed no duty to protect this citizen's property. Case dismissed.

## Throat Cut In Police Custody... Police Liable

Leigh Ann Davis and her boyfriend Louis Jackson, Jr. got into a fight one evening around midnight.[8] A neighbor summoned police by dialing 911, and she reported that Leigh Ann was injured. Two city police officers arrived and found Leigh Ann on a porch bleeding and crying. They found Louis walking away from the porch, arrested and handcuffed him behind his back, and seated him on the curb facing the street. The officers called for a police van to take Louis to the police station.

---

[7] The facts and law of this case are set forth in *Robertson v. City of Topeka*, 644 P.2d 458 (Kan. 1982).

[8] The facts and law of this case are set forth in *Jackson v. City of Kansas City*, 947 P.2d 31 (Kan. 1997).

Both Louis and Leigh Ann had been drinking. Nobody mentioned to the police that Leigh Ann had a box knife in her jeans pocket. Leigh Ann was seated somewhere behind Louis. Officer Crockett was standing in the street about two feet in front of Louis, while Officer Anderson was to Louis' right. Both officers were writing in their notebooks, using flashlights to do so.

Leigh Ann got up and moved toward Louis. Officer Crockett stopped her and placed her away at a distance from Louis. Officer Crockett returned to the curb area near Louis. He heard a sound, looked up, and saw Leigh Ann pull Louis' head back. She then sliced Louis's throat ear to ear with her box knife. The officers were close enough to have prevented the attack; after it they forcibly disarmed Leigh Ann.

Louis sued the police department for negligently failing to protect him while he was handcuffed, defenseless, and in police custody. A jury heard the case and awarded Louis $158,000 in damages. The Kansas Supreme Court affirmed that jury verdict and award, holding that the police did owe a duty to protect Louis in this situation.

Imagine that the government and the police have rendered you defenseless, and yet you remain in danger of violent attack. Will the possibility of your suing the police, if they fail to protect you, make you any safer?

# Commonwealth of Kentucky

The Court of Appeals of Kentucky has clearly declined to impose a duty on police to protect individual citizens, where it has stated:

> The general rule of thumb, in the absence of some "special relationship," is that a municipality or a law enforcement agency or official does not owe individual citizens a duty to protect them from crime.[1]

Kentucky follows this rule because "the duty to protect is owed to the public as a whole rather than to a particular individual or class of citizens, and [the rule] recognizes the existence of resource allocation."[2] The effect of the rule is that courts will usually dismiss a citizen's claim that the police failed to protect him; the courts will not even "consider the 'reasonableness' of actions taken to protect individual citizens from crime."[3]

The Supreme Court of Kentucky has stated the law does not hold government to a high standard of performance of its protective functions:

> [A] city's relationship to individuals and to the public is not the same as if the city itself were a private individual or corporation, and its duties are

---

[1] *Ashby v. City of Louisville*, 841 S.W.2d 184, 189 (Ky. App. 1992).
[2] *Id.*
[3] *Id.*

not the same. When [the city] undertakes measures for the protection of its citizens, it is not to be held to the same standards of performance that would be required of a professional organization hired to do the job.[4]

Unmistakably the high court declared that a city has no enforceable duty to provide police or fire protection:

[W]hen a city provides police or fire protection... the degree of success that should or will be attained in any particular instance cannot be guaranteed, nor can it be defined in terms of duties. A city cannot be held liable for its omission to do all the things that could or should have been done in an effort to protect life and property.[5]

The Kentucky legislature has affirmed that the Commonwealth of Kentucky (the state government) retains its immunity from civil lawsuits except in certain specified situations.[6] In these specified situations, the citizens may not sue but must file their with the state Board of Claims.[7] In particular, the Commonwealth cannot be sued or otherwise held liable for its "discretionary acts or decisions," "executive decisions," "ministerial acts," "performance

---

[4]*Frankfort Variety, Inc. v. City of Frankfort*, 552 S.W.2d 653, 655 (Ky. 1977), *overruled in part, Gas Service Co v. City of London*, 687 S.W. 2d 144 (Ky. 1985).

[5]*Frankfort Variety*, 552 S.W.2d at 655.

[6]Ky. Rev. Stat. § 44.072.

[7]Ky. Rev. Stat. § 44.073; *Franklin County v. Malone*, 957 S.W.2d 195, 202-03 (Ky. 1997).

of obligations running to the public as a whole," and "performance of a self-imposed protective function to the public or citizens."[8] A county enjoys generally the same legal protection from lawsuits as does the state.[9]

To date there has been no judicial opinion showing how to apply these rules to a case where a citizen relies on dialing 911 for protection from crime. Based on the legislation and court language currently in force, would you trade your right to self-defense for a Kentucky government's plan to protect you from violent attack?

---

[8]Ky. Rev. Stat. § 44.074 (13)(a-e).
[9]*Franklin County*, 957 S.W.2d at 203.

# State of Louisiana

Louisiana law has roots in the Napoleonic Code of France, but that fact does not much affect whether police owe a citizen protection from criminal attack. The state constitution allows citizens to sue the state and local governments for cases involving contract disputes or tort claims.[1] A statute expressly allows such suits as well.[2] Ordinarily a citizen who sues a governmental entity does not get a jury trial.[3]

Citizens cannot sue the governmental entities, however, when a government official carries out a discretionary duty in a negligent way.[4] Public entities and officials cannot be held liable for negligently performing or failing to perform policy making or discretionary acts.[5]

Louisiana courts say that they do not follow a blanket "no-duty" rule.[6] Whether the police owe a duty to an individual victim, as opposed to the general public, is analyzed by the courts on a case-by-case basis. The courts nevertheless do look at cases using the "public duty" approach.

Under Louisiana law, "the duty of members of the police department is essentially that of maintaining peace and order, preventing and detecting crime and enforcing the law."[7] The police owe a "special duty" to

---

[1]La. Const. art. 12 § 10(A).

[2]La. Rev. Stat. Ann. § 39:1538.

[3]La. Rev. Stat. Ann. § 13:5105.

[4]La. Rev. Stat. Ann. § 39:1538.

[5]La. Rev. Stat. Ann. § 9:2798.1(B).

[6]*Hardy v. Bowie*, 719 So. 2d 1158, 1161 (La. App. 1998).

[7]*Barry v. Dennis*, 633 So. 2d 806, 809 (La. App. 1994).

an individual only when (1) there is a specific written law that imposes a duty to protect a class of individuals, or (2) there is a "personal relationship" or "one-to-one relationship" between the individual and the police.[8] Whether there is such a "one-to-one" relationship between the individual and the police depends, for example, on the "closeness and proximity in time" between the police officer's actions and the individual's harm.[9]

Beyond the question of duty is the question of immunity, i.e. whether a citizen can sue the governmental entity at all. The government cannot be sued for negligence in making policy or performing discretionary acts. What kind of conduct constitutes policy making or a discretionary act? It is not easy to answer this question standing alone.

To discover whether the police owe a duty to provide police protection or respond to a 911 call, consider the following cases:

◆  ◆  ◆

Two men, Bowie and Hardy, had been fighting on August 21, 1993, in Lafayette, Louisiana.[10] Upwards of 500 people were in the bars on the "Strip,"and four police officers and four off-duty sheriff's deputies were in the area helping to close the bars for the night. A gun shot was heard, and several officers moved through the crowds in the direction of the shot. They stopped, however, to investigate and break up a fight

---

[8]*Hardy*, 719 So. 2d at 1161.

[9]*Hardy*, 719 So. 2d at 1161.

[10]The facts and law of this case are set forth in *Hardy v. Bowie*, 719 So. 2d 1158 (La. App. 1998).

between 30 white men and one black man. When two more gun shots were heard, the officers made their way to the area and found Hardy shot.

The state court of appeal held that the evidence was too inconsistent and conflicting to decide whether the city police owed a duty to protect Hardy (because of a one-to-one relationship) or were immune from suit because of their performing a discretionary function. The court remanded the case to the lower court for a trial.

◆ ◆ ◆

Mrs. Ardoin filed for divorce and obtained a temporary restraining order against her husband on April 20, 1993.[11] The next day she got a court order to evict him from the former family home. Mr. Ardoin came to the home on April 22 to collect his things. An argument started, she asked him to leave and she called the police. Mr. Ardoin left the house and waited by his truck. When the police arrived, both individuals told the police that Mr. Ardoin had come to retrieve his belongings. Mrs. Ardoin informed the police about the restraining order, and the officers convinced Mr. Ardoin to leave.

Later that evening, Mrs. Ardoin called the chief of police to ask why the officers had not arrested Mr. Ardoin for violating the restraining order. She also told the chief that she didn't then want Mr. Ardoin arrested. On the evening of April 23, Mr. Ardoin came to the house and shot Mrs. Ardoin twice.

---

[11]The facts and law of this case are set forth in *Ardoin v. City of Mamou*, 685 So. 2d 294 (La. App. 1996).

A judge heard the case and entered judgment of $150,995.00 for Mrs. Ardoin against Mr. Ardoin (only). Mrs. Ardoin appealed the judgment, arguing that the city was also negligent and should be held responsible for paying the damages. The court of appeal upheld the judgment because the city owed no duty to arrest Mr. Ardoin for violating the restraining order.

There was no law requiring police to arrest persons who violate restraining orders, unless the police actually witness the violation. Also, there was no "closeness and proximity in time" between the failure to arrest and Mrs. Ardoin's injuries the following day. The police had received no other information to suggest that Mr. Ardoin posed such a grave danger to Mrs. Ardoin. All of these factors suggested that the police owed no special duty to protect Mrs. Ardoin.

The result: Mrs. Ardoin had a large judgment against Mr. Ardoin who probably could not pay it. The city would not be held liable to pay any part of the judgment.

♦  ♦  ♦

A drug deal went sour at about 9:45 p.m. on September 20, 1988, and two white women fired shots which killed a black man who was not involved in the transaction.[12] Police arrived and arrested the two women. Meanwhile, a crowd gathered and violence erupted. A riot ensued during which rioters threw rocks and bottles at police and firefighters. Fire erupted in nearby brush. As firefighters attempted to put it out, they were pelted by heavy debris. The police chief

---

[12]The facts and law of this case are set forth in *Kniepp v. City of Shreveport*, 609 So. 2d 1163 (La. App. 1992).

ordered all law enforcement and firefighting personnel to pull out of the area and form an outer perimeter. Rioters filled the void and set fire to buildings. More gun fire was heard. The police held back as the destruction mounted.

The owners of one of the buildings, in which the police had initially held the two arrested women for a time, sued the city for the property damage. The owners argued that the police and police chief had acted negligently, which resulted in their building being burned by the rioters. Both the trial court and the state court of appeal agreed, however, that the city police owed no legal duty to protect the owners' building. The decisions of the chief of police were "discretionary" and thus he and the city were immune from suit. Case dismissed.

♦   ♦   ♦

Wanda and Carl Zeagler had a marital spat one evening and Wanda left to stay at her friend Susan's house.[13] James, a male friend, joined the women and they went shopping and partying till the early morning hours. The group returned to Susan's house, but they moved Wanda's car so that it was parked behind a doctor's office in town. Susan then went to sleep while James and Wanda talked until dawn. Then Wanda and James retired to a bedroom.

Meanwhile, Wanda's husband Carl discovered where Wanda was, and that she was with another man. He was not "fooled by the old car at the doctor's office routine." Carl asked the sheriff to go with him to

---

[13]The facts and law of this case are set forth in *Zeagler v. Town of Jena*, 556 So. 2d 978 (La. App. 1990).

Susan's house to witness his wife's conduct, but the sheriff refused. Carl asked a patrolman friend to do it, and even offered the friend $500.00 to go with him and take pictures, but the patrolman refused. Carl asked the chief of police to help him get his wife Wanda out of Susan's house, but the chief said he could not do so without a warrant. Carl then said he would take care of the matter himself and drove away.

The chief and the patrolman, however, were worried about what Carl might do, so they also drove to Susan's house. They saw Carl trying to get into the front door. The chief told Carl to stop, but Carl ran around to the side of the house. The chief started after Carl, pausing only to tell the patrolman to radio for backup.

Carl broke into a side window, entered the house, and found Susan and James naked in bed and looking shocked. Carl shot Susan in the left buttock, shot James in the right buttock, and fired a third shot which missed James's groin and lodged in his leg. The chief got into the house and arrested Carl.

Susan sued the police for failing to warn the people in Susan's house when they knew Carl was angry and coming over, and for failing to stop Carl from entering the house and committing his violent acts. The state court of appeal upheld the dismissal of her claim against the police for two main reasons. First, before Carl actually broke into her home, the police owed no duty to protect Susan from Carl, because there was no statute that required the police to arrest Carl or take any other specific action. Second, there was no "one-to-one relationship" between the police and the Susan, and therefore they owed no duty to protect or warn her individually.

At only one point, when the police were actively trying to stop Carl from entering Susan's house, did the police owe a duty to act reasonably to prevent harm to Susan. The court held, however, that the police had acted reasonably when trying to catch and stop Carl after he broke in. Case dismissed.

♦   ♦   ♦

In Louisiana, if you are a potential victim who faces imminent criminal attack, then you have three practical choices: (1) dial 911 and wait for help, (2) call a lawyer and ask for a legal opinion about whether the police owe any duty to protect you, or (3) defend yourself with arms. Which choice makes sense to you?

# State of Maine

The Maine Tort Claims Act[1] protects governmental entities from lawsuits on any tort claim for damages, with a few exceptions. There is a $300,000 limit on any payment by a governmental entity to a citizen who successfully sues, unless there is an insurance policy that allows a higher payment.[2] Specific statutes immunize governmental entities[3] and their employees[4] from being held liable for negligence in the performing or failing to perform a "discretionary" function.

To date the Maine Supreme Court has not decided whether a police department or city has a duty to protect or rescue a person who calls 911 in an emergency. Two decisions in other cases suggest that the police owe no legal duty under Maine law to protect citizens against crime.

## *Sorry, Lady... Take A Hike*

Early in the morning of April 9, 1988, the Lewiston police stopped a car and arrested the driver for drunk driving and driving without a valid license.[5] Patti Moore was a passenger in that car. The driver told the police that he didn't want Patti to drive his car, so the police took him away with his car keys. The police did not give Patti a ride, so she started walking home.

---

[1] Maine Rev. Stat. Ann. tit. 14, §§ 8101 - 8119.

[2] Maine Rev. Stat. Ann. tit. 14, §§ 8105, 8116.

[3] Maine Rev. Stat. Ann. tit. 14, § 8104-B(3).

[4] Maine Rev. Stat. Ann. tit. 14, § 8111(1)(C).

[5] The facts and law of this case are set forth in *Moore v. City of Lewiston*, 596 A.2d 612 (Me. 1991).

As Patti was walking in the dark night, she was attacked and robbed by two assailants. She received injuries to her head, face, wrist and fingers, and suffered pain, blackouts, dysfunction of her arm and hand, and emotional distress that lasted for years.

Patti sued the city and the two officers for failing to protect her under the circumstances. The state Supreme Court held that she could only sue the city if the city had a valid insurance policy that covered her claim. The police officers themselves could not be sued, because the state law granted them absolute immunity.

## *Didn't Ask If Suicidal... No Duty*

John Doucette's father, Lucien, called the Lewiston police to report that John had taken his uncle's car, John was depressed and "full of" medication, the car had an unloaded rifle in the trunk, and nobody knew where John had gone.[6] Lucien asked if it were possible to have John picked up and checked into a detox center. The police dispatcher checked on the vehicle identification, but took no other action. In particular, the dispatcher did not input John's name into the national crime data base.

Later the same day, November 20, 1993, John was involved in an auto accident. The policeman thought John looked ill, and recommended John check into a motel to rest. A check of John's driver's license revealed nothing noteworthy. The next day, John was found dead, having committed suicide.

---

[6]The facts and law of this case are set forth in *Doucette v. City of Lewiston*, 697 A.2d 1292 (Me. 1997).

John's widow sued the dispatcher and city for (1) the dispatcher's failure to ask Lucien questions about whether John was suicidal (which was a required procedure) and (2) the dispatcher's failure to send out a missing person report on the national crime data base (which would have alerted the policeman who checked John's license).

The trial court dismissed Mrs. Doucette's lawsuit on a motion before trial, and the state Supreme Judicial Court affirmed that ruling. Under Maine law, the dispatcher's duties, such as checking John's potential for suicide and reporting John missing on the database, are "discretionary functions." The dispatcher could not be sued for negligently failing to carry out these duties because the dispatcher was "absolutely immune" from liability for such failure. As the dispatcher was not liable, neither was the city who employed the dispatcher.

Many other states have held that police response to 911 calls is a "discretionary function." If Maine courts adopt that position, then the police could escape legal liability for failing to respond to your 911 call. Should you rely on dialing 911 as your one and only emergency response to violent crime?

# State of Maryland

In Maryland, the law protects police agencies and the State from liability when they fail to protect citizens from criminals. As early as 1856, the United States Supreme Court held that a Maryland sheriff who failed to protect the public was subject to discipline or criminal charges, but would not be held liable to the private citizen who suffered damage.[1] Similarly, a sheriff who failed to protect a prisoner in custody from a lynch mob was held immune from civil suit in 1898.[2]

## *Millham is Drunk-Driving and Dangerous... So What?*

One evening a police officer found John Millham, drunk, sitting behind the wheel in his pickup truck with its lights on and engine running.[3] Under Maryland law, the police officer could have arrested Millham and charged him with drunken driving. The officer, however, merely told Millham to park his truck and not drive any more that night. When the officer left, Millham drove his truck a short distance, then crashed into John Ashburn's car.

Ashburn tried to sue the officer, the police department, and the county, to recover damages for the leg he lost and other injuries he suffered due to the collision with Millham. Ashburn argued that the police

---

[1] *South v. Maryland*, 59 U.S. 396, 403 (1856).

[2] *Cocking v. Wade*, 40 A. 104 (Md. 1898).

[3] The facts and law of this case are set forth in *Ashburn v. Anne Arundel County*, 510 A.2d 1078 (Md. 1986).

had a legal duty to have arrested Millham or otherwise stopped him from driving drunk.

The Maryland Court of Appeals, the state's highest court, refused to permit Ashburn's suit to go forward. The Court held that the police owed a "duty," because of their public office, to protect the *public* but not private individuals. The only suitable punishment for police negligence is an administrative sanction, or possibly criminal charges. The victim of the police negligence would have no legal claim unless the policeman had taken custody of the wrongdoer or had been in control of the dangerous actor.

The same rule would apply to any case in which the police failed to protect a citizen from criminal activity.

## *Victims Get No "Due Process" Right to Protection*

When the police fail to protect you, can you sue them for denying your civil rights? In a Maryland case which the judges called "genuinely tragic," the Fourth Circuit Court of Appeals answered "no."

Officer Johnson arrested Don Pittman on March 10, 1989, after Carol Pinder called to report Pittman's breaking in, screaming, and pushing and punching her, as well as threatening her children.[4] Pittman, who had recently been released from prison for attempted arson of Carol's home, reportedly had threatened to murder the whole family

After Carol told the policeman that she was afraid of Pittman coming back to harm her and her children,

---

[4]The facts and law of this case are set forth in *Pinder v. Johnson*, 54 F.3d 1169 (4th Cir. 1995) *(en banc)*.

Officer Johnson assured her that Pittman would be locked up all night. Carol relied on Officer Johnson's words, left her children home, and went to work that night.

Officer Johnson, however, charged Pittman with simple misdemeanors only, not more serious crimes, so the county commissioner released Pittman with a warning to stay away from Carol Pinder's home. Pittman returned that night to set fire to the Pinders' house while Carol was away; the smoke killed her three children sleeping inside.

Carol sued the police and the government to recover damages for herself and for the wrongful deaths of her children. She argued that the police and the commissioner had denied her and her children their "due process" civil right to protection. No such luck, the court said, because the policeman had no "clearly established" duty to protect individual citizens like the Pinders. Following U.S. Supreme Court precedent, the court held that the Due Process Clause of the Constitution does not require the state to provide any particular protection to citizens. Therefore the state was not liable under the Due Process Clause in this case where the state had chosen not to protect an individual, and the individual suffered harm as a result.

## Protection Under the Riot Act

A Maryland statute allows citizens who suffer damage during a riot to sue the city to recoup their losses.[5] To win under that statute (called the "Riot Act"), the citizen must prove: 1) the city had good

---

[5]Md. Ann. Code art. 82, § 2 (Michie 1991).

reasons to believe that a riot was about to take place, or (2) the city had notice of a riot in time to prevent property destruction, and (3) having notice, the city had the ability by itself (or with its own citizens) to prevent the damage. If the city "uses all reasonable diligence and all powers entrusted to it for the prevention or suppression of riots," however, then the city will not be liable to the citizens.[6]

Note that the citizen must prove that a "riot" did take place, not just some ordinary group crime.[7] Assuming the citizen can prove all facts necessary for the Riot Act claim, and is willing to pay all the costs and attorneys fees and suffer several years of stress while the judicial procedures grind away, then the citizen might receive some money for the city's failure to prevent or quell a riot—long after the fact.

---

[6]*Mayor and City Council of Baltimore v. Silver*, 283 A.2d 788, 790 n.2 (Md. 1971).

[7]18A E. McQuillin, *The Law of Municipal Corporations* § 53.148 (3d ed. 1993).

# Commonwealth of Massachusetts

Under Massachusetts law a citizen cannot sue the government for failing "to provide adequate police protection, prevent the commission of crimes, investigate, detect or solve crimes, identify or apprehend criminals or suspects, arrest or detain suspects, or enforce any law..."[1] Neither can citizens sue when the state releases a criminal on parole or furlough from prison.[2]

Moreover, citizens cannot sue the government for failing to "prevent or diminish the harmful consequences of... the violent or tortious conduct of a third person [who is not a government employee]."[3] This law generally precludes lawsuits that claim the police failed to protect any particular person from criminal aggression. The exceptions which allow a person to sue include cases where:[4]

(1) the police give "explicit and specific assurances of safety or assistance" to the direct victim of such aggression (or his family), and the victim suffered harm in part because he relied on those assurances; or

(2) the police action puts the victim in a worse position than before the action.

---

[1] Mass. Gen. Laws Ann. ch. 258, § 10(h).

[2] *Id.*, § 10(I).

[3] *Id.*, § 10(j).

[4] *Id.*, § 10(j)(1-2).

Whether or not a person can sue the police depends upon whether the police owe an enforceable legal duty to that person. But what if the victim has a court order against the attacker, has reported dozens of violations of that court order, and for 15 months the police do nothing about it?

## *Police Advised: "Get A Gun"...*
## *She Dialed 911 Instead*

James Davidson had been abusing and harassing his wife, Catherine Ford, after their separation.[5] Catherine got a court order against James on October 18, 1984, to stop his misconduct. A court order is merely a piece of paper until the police enforce it, so Catherine had to deliver it that day to the Grafton police station and have it served on James. Knowing James's history of violent conduct, a Grafton police officer told Catherine then that the police could not babysit her twenty-four hours a day. The officer advised her to "buy a gun because the only way to deal with violence is violence."

She did not take that advice. Over the next 15 months, James continued to harass and stalk Catherine, and he repeatedly threatened to kill her and her family. Trying to apply the power of the court order, Catherine continually reported these threats to the Grafton police. The police told her that they could not do anything until James caused her some actual physical harm. To respond to James's telephonic terrorism, the police often suggested that Catherine "get a gun or call the telephone company."

---

[5]The facts and law of this case are set forth in *Ford v. Town of Grafton*, 693 N.E.2d 1047 (Mass. App. 1998).

Catherine and others of her family called the Grafton police dozens of times to report James' stalking, threatening, and harassing behavior. One time James threatened to kidnap Catherine's sister's infant child, but the police did nothing. Another time James's own psychiatrist warned Catherine that James had plans to kill her. Several times James came to Catherine's or her family's residence to terrorize her. He attacked her at her workplace. He was caught once sneaking in the back yard and admitted that he had violated the court order. Despite all of his vicious and unlawful behavior, the police never arrested James for violating the court order.

James issued his final death threat on January 16, 1986. Catherine reported this threat to the police. At about 6:00 p.m. the next evening, James starting kicking down Catherine's back door. She ran out the front door. James saw her and chased her even as she charged through moving traffic on the street. She pounded on a neighbor's door, but no one would let her inside. As she ran to the next house, James caught her and shot her three times in the face and neck. He then shot himself. Catherine was totally paralyzed for life.

Catherine sued the town of Grafton for failing to protect her. Her lawyers argued that the police owed a legal duty to stop James, and thus the police owed a legal duty to protect Catherine. A Massachusetts statute required the police to arrest James for his repeated violations of the court order, but the police had failed to arrest him.[6]

---

[6]Mass. Gen. Laws Ann. ch. 209A §§ 6-7, *cited in Ford*, 693

The Massachusetts courts applied the immunity statute to shield the city from liability. The court order that was supposed to restrain James and protect Catherine did not amount to an "assurance of safety or assistance" from the police department. The fact that the police advised Catherine "to get a gun for protection" showed that the police were unable to assure her safety or protect her.[7]

No duty to protect, therefore no lawsuit. Fully 11 years after she filed her suit against the city, the Massachusetts court of appeal dismissed her case entirely.[8]

Catherine Ford would likely have escaped James's murderous intentions unharmed if she had taken the police officer's advice to "get a gun" and had received a basic course in defensive firearms handling and safety. Tragically, she chose instead to rely on a court order and dialing 911.

Would you make the same mistake?

---

N.E.2d at 1052 n. 6.

[7]*Ford*, 693 N.E.2d at 1054.

[8]Catherine Ford had also sued the city for violating her civil and constitutional rights by not protecting her. The court dismissed those claims as well. *Id.* at 1055-57.

# State of Michigan

The Michigan legislature passed a law to make sure that police departments would not be held liable for failing to protect individual citizens in most cases.[1] Michigan state and local governments who commit negligence while doing something for profit (not taxes or fees) can be liable for damages they cause.[2] As a government agency, however, the police department *cannot* be liable for damages it causes by negligently carrying out a "governmental function."[3] A "governmental function" is "any activity which is expressly or impliedly mandated or authorized by constitution, statute, or other law."[4]

In practice, how much does Michigan law protect potential crime victims?

## *Priority Zero*

As he walked past the doorway of his parents' home, Elvera Trezzi sensed something was very wrong.[5] Through the window he saw their refrigerator door was open, and lights inside the home were off. Elvera called 911 six times that day, April 23, 1978.

---

[1] *See* Mich. Comp. Laws § 691.1401 *et seq.*, Mich. Stat. Ann. § 3.996(101) *et seq.*

[2] *Ross v. Consumers Power Co.*, 363 N.W.2d 641, 647 (Mich. 1984).

[3] Id.

[4] Id.

[5] The facts of this case are set forth in *Trezzi v. Detroit*, 328 N.W.2d 70 (Mich. App. 1982) and in *Ross*, 363 N.W.2d at 651-52, 699-700 (affirming *Trezzi* decision).

The 911 operators assigned a low priority to Elvera's calls and passed them on to the police dispatcher. The police dispatcher delayed sending out a unit, and even allowed the policemen to take lunch before responding to the calls. Ninety precious minutes elapsed before the police unit was sent to scene.

Before Elvera had called, an unknown attacker had already broken into the home. While Elvera was dialing 911 and during the 90 minute dispatcher delay, the attacker murdered both of his parents.

Elvera sued the city police department. The trial court dismissed his lawsuit without a trial; the Court of Appeals of Michigan affirmed that decision, as did the Michigan Supreme Court. "[T]he categorizing of emergency calls by a 911 operator and the dispatch of police vehicles" based on that operator's judgment "are activities which are expressly or impliedly mandated or authorized" by Michigan law.[6] Because of this fact, the 911 operator was performing "a governmental function" for the city and the police. Therefore, according to the state Supreme Court, "the city is entitled to governmental immunity."[7]

While Elvera was dialing 911 and relying upon the police to respond, his parents were murdered by an attacker. The 911 system had placed a low priority on their lives. Elvera couldn't even sue for damages afterward, because the bureaucratic mistake was "immune" from suit.

---

[6] *Ross,* 363 N.W.2d at 676-77.
[7] *Id.* at 677.

## New Motto: "To Watch & To Wait" ?

Even when the police are watching a brawl, they owe no duty to protect any particular individual citizens whether or not they are directly involved. In one Detroit case, two officers sat in their marked police car and watched while a fight erupted outside a bar.[8] The officers did call for additional police help, but they themselves did nothing else to break up the fight. The officers did not even move their car closer to the spot, sound their siren, or do anything to make themselves seen. One of the brawlers shot a bystander whose brother was in the fight.

The Michigan courts held that the policemen as individuals, and the city police, enjoyed governmental immunity and could not be sued for failing to stop the fight or protect the bystander. The officers owed a duty to protect "the public generally" but not to protect any particular individual. Under Michigan law, officers faced with a potentially dangerous decision had to "be given a wide degree of discretion" in deciding what to do... even if their decision was to sit idly in their police car watching on-going violence and waiting for "backup."

In Michigan, "governmental immunity" means no guarantee of police protection. You have to protect yourself.[9]

---

[8]The facts and law of this case are set forth in *Zavala v. Zinser*, 333 N.W.2d 278 (Mich. App. 1983), *affirmed in Ross*, 363 N.W.2d at 678-79.

[9]After the *Ross* and *Zavala* decisions, the Michigan legislature in 1986 amended the statutes to strengthen the protection of individual government employees from liability. The amended statutes also allow a private citizen to sue a government agency,

such as the police, but only if that agency has acted with "gross negligence." The agency would be acting with "gross negligence" if its conduct was "so reckless as to demonstrate a substantial lack of concern for whether an injury results." *See Haberl v. Rose*, 570 N.W.2d 664, 671 (Mich. App. 1997)(quoting the statute); *see also Hickey v. Zezulka*, 487 N.W.2d 106 (Mich. 1992)(broad governmental immunity still applies).

# State of Minnesota

Citizens of Minnesota can sue the state[1] and the municipal[2] governments for negligence in many cases. State law prohibits any suits, however, which claim that the government or its employees improperly performed or failed to perform "a discretionary function or duty."[3]

The law is not simple to apply. For example, when a social worker develops a case plan to monitor a case of child abuse in the home, the county social worker has performed "a discretionary duty."[4] The social worker and the county government cannot be held liable if the plan is poor. Carrying out that plan, however, is not a "discretionary duty," so the social worker and county can be liable for her negligence in implementing the plan.[5]

Where do emergency calls to 911 fit into Minnesota's legal scheme? It is a "fundamental principle," wrote one Minnesota court, that "a municipality cannot be held liable for failing to supply general police or fire protection."[6] Generally, police officers exercising their official duties are performing

---

[1] Minn. Stat. Ann. § 3.736.

[2] Minn. Stat. Ann § 466.02.

[3] Minn. Stat. Ann § 466.03; Minn. Stat. Ann. § 3.736.

[4] *Olson v. Ramsey County*, 509 N.W.2d 368, 371-72 (Minn. 1993).

[5] *Id.* at 372.

[6] *Dahlheimer v. City of Dayton*, 441 N.W.2d 534, 537 (Minn. App. 1989).

"discretionary duties," and therefore are usually immune from liability.[7]

## *"We haven't got enough police, you know..."*

Mr. & Mrs. Silver operated Silver's Food Market in the Plymouth Avenue North area of Minneapolis.[8] On July 19, 1967, a riot broke out in that area and the store's windows were broken. The Silvers reported their damage to the police, but actually they had been lucky. Other stores in the area had been damaged and looted.

The Silvers saw that the rioting was not over, and they had received threats that their store would be further damaged, so they boarded up the windows. Mr. Silvers called the police to report the threats. According to Mr. Silvers, the police responded: "We know about it and we are going to have some extra police to guard Plymouth Avenue, but we haven't got enough police, you know, to watch every business place in Plymouth.... [W]e are going to keep an eye on your place, but we cannot give you special protection."[9]

Rioters hurled "Molotov cocktails" at Silver's Food Market the next night, and the store burned. The Silvers sued the City of Minneapolis for failing to provide both police and fire protection to their building after they had requested it, and for failing to act reasonably to prevent the riot.

---

[7] *Leonzal v. Grogan*, 516 N.W.2d 210, 213 (Minn. App. 1994).

[8] The facts and law of this case are set forth in *Silver v. City of Minneapolis*, 170 N.W.2d 206 (Minn. 1969).

[9] *Id.* at 207.

The trial court dismissed the Silvers' case, and the state Supreme Court agreed. Providing police and fire protection are "discretionary" functions. The city cannot be sued for negligently failing to carry out discretionary functions. The Supreme Court of Minnesota declared the law that applied to the Silvers:

> We think it is enough to say that here, in the light of rumored impending riots, the city had the right to decide how most effectively to deploy its police and fire manpower so as to control such riots to the best of its ability if they did break out, and to furnish protection to as many citizens as its manpower would permit. [The Silvers] were not entitled to more protection than others.[10]

The police cannot do everything and be everywhere. Citizens should not expect any special protection from the police.

## The 911 Call That Went Too Far

Mr. & Mrs. Leonzal did not get along with their neighbors.[11] The two households argued about parking arrangements. Relations worsened when the neighbors' dog bit the Leonzal's child in their own yard. When the Leonzals started to build a fence between the properties, the neighbors disputed the property line. When the Leonzals painted an orange boundary line on the grass, the neighbors retaliated by throwing bricks

---

[10]*Id.* at 209.

[11]The facts and law of this case are set forth in *Leonzal v. Grogan*, 516 N.W.2d 210 (Minn. App. 1994).

and sticks into the Leonzals' yard. Once the fence was built, the neighbors' dog dug under it, and mysteriously the Leonzals' flower garden was destroyed.

Both the Leonzals and the neighbors had called the police many times, and the Leonzals had filed five formal complaints with the city attorney. The situation escalated when, on August 31, 1989, the neighbors called 911 to report that Mr. Leonzal was waving a shotgun outside his home and threatening the life of the neighbor and her dog.

The police responded immediately by sending several squad cars to the site. They set up outside the Leonzals' house with guns drawn. A desk sergeant telephoned Mr. Leonzal inside his home, told him about the complaint and that there were police officers outside, and asked him to go outside to talk to the officers. Mr. Leonzal became angry on the phone, denied the neighbors' accusation, and said that he and his wife had been having a relaxing evening at home. He then went outside and shouted at the officers. The officers told him to "freeze" and put his hands on his head, but Leonzal kept shouting at them. The officers told him to lie face down but he refused. They forced him down, handcuffed him, and put him into the squad car.

It turned out that Mr. Leonzal did not even own a shotgun, but did own several hunting rifles. He told police where they were, and they found those weapons without further incident.

Arguing that the police had negligently overreacted to the neighbors' false report, the Leonzals sued the police for battering him and emotionally traumatizing him. The neighbors had previously phoned in false 911 calls, and the police knew it, so the police should not have come down so hard on Mr. Leonzal on this bogus "emergency."

The state appeals court held that "[a]n officer's response to a 911 call involves the exercise of discretion." This is particularly true where the call involves "an armed person threatening the life of a neighbor." Accordingly, under the doctrine of "official immunity," neither the police nor the city could be held liable to the Leonzals.

Under Minnesota law, it seems that when someone dials 911, the police are shielded from liability for failing to protect victims... regardless of whether the police fail to respond or they respond too aggressively.

# State of Mississippi

The Mississippi legislature has declared that the state and its municipal governments "are, always have been and shall continue to be immune from suit... on account of any wrongful or tortious act or omission..."[1] The legislature does allow persons to sue the state and the cities for torts, however, up to a limit of $500,000 or the amount of their insurance, whichever is greater.[2]

Even so, citizens cannot bring a legal action against the state or city governments "arising out of any act or omission of any employee of a governmental entity engaged in the performance... of duties or activities relating to police or fire protection unless the employee acted in reckless disregard of the safety and well-being of" a person not committing a crime at the time.[3] Also, citizens cannot sue the government for damages resulting from "riots" or other "civil disturbances."[4]

Mississippi's courts apply the law strictly. In one case, a house caught fire and the fire department was called.[5] The nearest fire hydrant was 1000 feet away, and nearest water main was over 3,500 feet away. The fire department responded, started to put out the flames, but ran out of water. As result, the homeowners suffered losses of $715,560.

---

[1]Miss. Code Ann. § 11-46-3(1).

[2]Miss. Code Ann. § 11-46-5 (waiver) , § 11-46-15 (limit), § 11-46-16 (insurance).

[3]Miss. Code Ann. § 11-46-9(1)(c).

[4]Miss. Code Ann. § 11-46-9(1)(u).

[5]The facts and law of this case are set forth in *Westbrook v. City of Jackson*, 665 So. 2d 833 (Miss. 1995).

The homeowners sued the city for failing to provide adequate fire protection service. Although a city law required the city to provide water lines for fire protection "where necessary and economically feasible," the city had not installed a sufficient system. That fact did not change the outcome of the case. "Sovereign immunity cloaks both the officials and the City of Jackson for any inadequacies in water service for fire protection," wrote the state Supreme Court.

In a different case, a police car in pursuit of a drunk driver crashed into an innocent bystander.[6] The state Supreme Court held that the police department is a "governmental function," and therefore the city was shielded from suit because of "sovereign immunity."

Governmental immunity in Mississippi means that the fire department owes no enforceable duty to provide adequate fire protection, and the police department owes no enforceable duty to protect individuals from harm. In that state, citizens had better plan to take care of themselves.

---

[6]The facts and law of this case are set forth in *Mosby v. Moore*, 716 So. 2d 551 (Miss. 1998).

# State of Missouri

State and local governmental entities in Missouri enjoy the protection of sovereign immunity, with a few exceptions such as motor vehicle accidents and injuries on public property.[1] Cities and their police departments are therefore not held liable if they negligently perform their "governmental functions" or "discretionary duties." Consider these two cases below.

## *Sorry, 911 Is Out of Order*

Eric Clark invaded the St. Louis home of several young women on May 15, 1984.[2] At about 2:30 a.m., Clark accosted one of the roommates outside and forced her to open the door to the shared apartment. Clark tied up all of the occupants, and then forced a young woman "R.C." (code-named to protect her privacy in the court system) to go with him while he searched the place for money. Then Clark sexually assaulted and raped R.C. in a bathroom.

Meanwhile, one of the other roommates escaped and secretly dialed 911. To avoid being overheard by the attacker, the roommate spoke too softly for the 911 operator to hear. As a result, the operator wrote down the wrong address and then dispatched an "all points bulletin" to alert police to a "hold-up" in progress.

The 911 operator suspected that the address was wrong, and so tried to call the apartment back. By then, however, the attacker had ripped out the

---

[1]Mo. Ann. Stat. § 537.600 (West Supp. 1999).

[2]The facts and law of this case are set forth in *R.C. v. Southwestern Bell Telephone Co.*, 759 S.W.2d 617 (Mo. App. 1988).

telephone wires. The operator called the telephone company special service number to obtain the address that matched the phone number. The special service operator reported, however, that "sorry our computers are down." The 911 operator had no other resources to obtain the correct address. Had the police been given the correct address, they could have arrived within two minutes of the initial call.

After the ordeal, R.C. sued the police, the city and the telephone company for negligently failing to provide an adequate 911 system. The system did not have enough amplification for soft voices, the operators were insufficiently trained, and the "back up" system for obtaining and verifying addresses was deficient.

Under the immunity statute, the state court of appeals held that the city could not be sued on R.C.'s claim. The police department officials could not be held liable for negligent performance of their duties, because operating a 911 system is a "discretionary" function. Government employees who perform "discretionary" duties are protected from suits by official immunity. Case dismissed.

Would Clark have invaded the women's apartment had he suspected that one of the occupants was armed? R.C. will never know. But she does know that dialing 911 can be absolutely pointless.

## *Police Allow Civilian Into On-going Crime Scene... No Duty*

The Italian Festival Committee contracted with the Kansas City government to permit their Festival to take place in a city park.[3] As a condition of the contract, however, the Committee had to hire off-duty police officers to provide security for the event.

The Committee hired Claudio Fantasma, Jr., to serve as Security Director for the Festival. While working with several off-duty police officers to secure the Festival grounds on September 27, 1991, Fantasma and the officers heard several gunshots. The officers decided to check out the problem, and Fantasma said he would go with them.

Just a short time later, some person fired several gunshots at the group. Fantasma was hit in the chest and died.

Fantasma's widow and her two daughters sued the city and the police. They argued that the police had a duty to protect Fantasma from harm in this case, and specifically to prevent him from going with the officers into a crime scene. The court held, however, that the city and the police were immune from this suit.

A Missouri statute required the police department "to preserve the public peace, prevent crime and arrest offenders, protect the rights of persons and property, and guard the public health."[4] That statute, however, imposed a duty on the police to protect the public generally, but not any particular individual. No police duty, no liability, no case.

Even when the police are with you in a dangerous situation, you cannot depend upon them to protect

---

[3]The facts and law of this case are set forth in *Fantasma v. Kansas City*, 913 S.W.2d 388 (Mo. App. 1996).

[4]Mo. Ann. Stat. § 84.420.1.

you... regardless of laws and regulations. When in doubt... think self-preservation!

# State of Montana

Montana is one state where statutes impose certain duties on the police, and citizens can sue the police for failing to carry out those duties. For example, one law requires the chief of police "to arrest all persons guilty of a breach of the peace or of the violation of any city or town ordinance..."[1] Another law imposes duties on a county sheriff to preserve the peace, to arrest all persons who attempt or have committed a public offense, and to prevent and suppress all riots and breaches of the peace.[2]

Montana law allows government to be sued for damages, unless otherwise specified by the legislature.[3] There is a limit on the amount that the government will pay on negligence claims: $750,000 per claim, with a cap of $1.5 million per occurrence (total payout for all persons' claims based on the same set of facts).[4]

## Bleeding in the Brain for Sixteen Hours In Jail... He Can Sue!

So far the Montana courts have enforced statutory duties against police departments. In one case, for example, a bar owner slammed a heavy metal bar into the skull of Jeffrey Azure.[5] Seven hours after attack, the

---

[1] Mont. Code Ann. § 7-32-4105(h).

[2] Mont. Code Ann. § 7-32-2121.

[3] Mont. Code Ann. § 2-9-102.

[4] Mont. Code Ann. § 2-9-108. A city can be liable for as much as its insurance policy allows, however, if the policy limits are larger than set forth in the statute.

[5] The facts and law of this case are set forth in *Azure v. City of Billings*, 596 P.2d 460 (Mont. 1979).

Billings city police responded to a call reporting a burglary, found Azure on the premises, and arrested him. Azure was charged with public intoxication and trespass, and thrown into jail.

Azure was not a pretty sight. Two black eyes, a large bruise on his forehead and dried blood on his lips and teeth, all suggested he had suffered a recent injury. The police ignored these signs for 16 hours. When the police finally took Azure to the hospital emergency room, he was semi-conscious.

Some thirty hours later the doctors discovered that he had suffered severe bleeding in the brain. Azure lost part of his sight and was permanently and totally disabled.

Azure sued the police department for failing to carry out a statutory duty. A Montana law required police to take persons who appear severely drunk into protective custody and then deliver them to a hospital for treatment.[6] In Azure's case, the police had arrested him for public drunkenness and could see that he was incapacitated, but had failed to get him prompt medical treatment as required by law.

The Supreme Court of Montana upheld Azure's right to sue.[7] A jury awarded Azure only $20,000 on his claim against the police department. There appears good reason to believe, however, that Montana courts will insist that local police carry out any existing statutory duties to protect individual citizens.

---

[6]Mont. Code Ann. § 53-24-303.

[7]*See also State of Montana v. District Court of the Thirteenth Judicial District*, 550 P.2d 382 (Mont. 1976) (City of Billings, but not the state government, could be liable for Azure's injuries).

Even when the police owe a legal duty, of course, that might simply mean that you (or your heirs) can sue the police *after* they fail. The fear of lawsuits might impel Montana police to pay a little more attention to their duties... but that extra motivation won't slow down the criminal who is invading your home at midnight....

# State of Nebraska

Two sets of statutes immunize the state[1] and local[2] governments of Nebraska from tort lawsuits for damages, but then permit citizens to bring a wide range of suits. Thus, the law directs the "state shall be liable in the same manner and to the same extent as a private individual under like circumstances."[3] The same basic rule applies to local governments.[4] Ironically, the person who sues a Nebraska government entity in such cases is *not* entitled to a jury trial.[5]

Citizens generally cannot sue the government or the police officers, however, for negligently performing a "discretionary function or duty."[6] It's not that the citizen cannot file the suit, but rather that the police generally owe no duty to protect individuals.[7] The reason the police owe no duty to protect, however, is that *no* individual has a duty "to control the conduct of a third person" and thereby prevent him from harming someone else.[8]

As with nearly every rule in law, exceptions to this police no-duty rule exist. Thus, when the police have

---

[1]Neb. Rev. Stat. Ann. § 81-8, 209 *et seq.*

[2]Neb. Rev. Stat. Ann. § 13-902 *et seq.*

[3]Neb. Rev. Stat. Ann. § 81-8,215.

[4]Neb. Rev. Stat. Ann. § 13-908.

[5]Neb. Rev. Stat. Ann. § 81-8,219(1) (state); Neb. Rev. Stat. Ann. § 13-910 (municipalities).

[6]Neb. Rev. Stat. Ann. § 81-8,214 (state); Neb. Rev. Stat. Ann. § 13-907 (municipalities).

[7]*Hamilton v. City of Omaha*, 498 N.W.2d 555, 560 (Neb. 1993).

[8]*Id.*, *citing* Restatement (Second) of Torts § 315 (1965).

specifically promised or started to protect a particular person, and that person has specifically relied on the police for that protection, then the police have a legally enforceable duty to provide that protection.[9] Typical situations of police duty would include: (1) when the police protect the particular person because he has helped the police as an informer or witness, and (2) when the police have expressly promised to protect the particular person from harm.[10]

Confused yet? Consider the following true life cases.

## *Officer Said He Would Be Around To Protect Her... No Duty*

Jeffrey Hamilton physically assaulted his former wife Saundra on January 14, 1988.[11] She then went back to her home. Police arrived shortly at the scene of the assault and learned from witnesses the identity of both Saundra and Jeffrey, and what had happened.

Twenty minutes after Saundra got home, Jeffrey came by and harassed and threatened her. She immediately called the police. Officer Green arrived just after Jeffrey had left. Saundra told the officer what had happened and requested special protection. Officer Green said that he would be on duty and in the immediate area to protect her. Saundra stayed in her home because of the officer's assurance.

---

[9]*Brandon v. County of Richardson*, 566 N.W.2d 776, 780 (Neb. 1997).

[10]*Id.*

[11]The facts and law of this case are set forth in *Hamilton v. City of Omaha*, 498 N.W.2d 555 (Neb. 1993).

About 20 more minutes later, Jeffrey returned, kicked down her door, and barged into Saundra's home. She called 911 to report the attack in progress. As she was trying to escape through another door, Jeffrey attacked her. She fled across the street trying to get a neighbor's help. Jeffrey caught her and bashed her arms and legs with a tire iron. He then dragged her down some stairs and dumped her on the concrete.

Saundra sued the police department because the officer had promised to protect her but failed to do so, and the result was a brutal attack with serious injuries. Five years after the attack, the Nebraska Supreme Court held that the law permitted Saundra to sue the police department, but that her claim lacked enough evidence to go to trial. Specifically, Saundra's claim lacked evidence that Officer Green had assured her that she could stay home. She also hadn't proved that she actually would have taken some other defensive action if Officer Green had not assured her.

Case dismissed.

## *Crime Victim/Witness Dies...*
## *Heirs Get A Lawsuit*

Two violent criminals abducted, imprisoned, assaulted and raped Teena Brandon on Christmas Day, 1993.[12] The attackers threatened to kill Teena if she reported the crime. Teena escaped from them, however, and reported the whole story to the sheriff, including the death threat. The sheriff directed his deputy to conduct an investigation, and delegated

---

[12]The facts and law of this case are set forth in *Brandon v. County of Richardson*, 566 N.W.2d 776 (Neb. 1997).

other parts of the investigation to another police department.

Teena thought the sheriff was going to arrest the two attackers she had named, so she stayed in town. Although the sheriff learned of physical evidence that supported Teena's report, the sheriff decided not to arrest the suspects. Instead, the other police department questioned the two suspects and released them. Teena was never told that the suspects had been questioned but not jailed. Unaware of these facts, Teena stayed in town rather than leaving the area.

The two criminals shot and killed Teena on December 31, 1993. Her heirs sued the county sheriff's department for failing to protect Teena under these circumstances. The Supreme Court of Nebraska held that Teena's heirs could receive damages from the county for having caused her wrongful death. Teena fell into the category of "informer or witness," and therefore the sheriff owed her a duty to protect her.

Too bad Teena relied on the police to protect her, instead of taking steps to protect herself.

# State of Nevada

Nevada has a long history of legalized casino-style gambling, but do you want to gamble your life that the police there will protect you? The Nevada state legislature has decreed that a citizen cannot sue a police officer, a police department, a municipality or the state for failing to provide security to a specific individual or group.[1] The Supreme Court of Nevada has ruled that, generally speaking, "government is not liable for failing to prevent the unlawful acts of others."[2]

As is true in most states, however, there is an exception that allows a citizen to sue if there was a "special relationship" between that citizen (victim) and the police which would require the police to protect that citizen.[3] Also, a crime victim can sue the police department for failing to protect her if an officer specifically promised help to her and she relied on that promise, or if the officer affirmatively caused the harm.[4] When the victim can sue the government under these situations, the maximum liability of the government is limited to $50,000.[5]

---

[1] See Nev. Rev. Stat. § 41.032(2), *quoted and applied in Bruttomesso v. Las Vegas Metropolitian Police Dept.*, 591 P.2d 254, 255 (Nev. 1979).

[2] *Bruttomesso,* 591 P.2d at 255.

[3] *Id.*

[4] Nev. Rev. Stat. § 41.0336; *see Snyder v. Viani*, 885 P.2d 610 (Nev. 1994) (statute does not eliminate rule that government owes protection to the public, not to individual persons).

[5] Nev. Rev. Stat. § 41.035.

What if the police refuse outright to provide security at a public event?

## A Hard Night's Day In Court

The Clark County Library was hosting a "Beatles" film festival, and requested the Las Vegas Metro police to provide security protection.[6] The police department denied the request because of "inadequate man power." Garry Bruttomesso attended the film festival, and was stabbed repeatedly by an attacker in the Library parking lot.

Bruttomesso sued the police department for damages. The Nevada Supreme Court applied the Nevada statute and the general rule to hold that providing police protection was a "discretionary function" of government, so the police could not be sued for negligently failing to carry out that function. Also, there was no "special relationship" between Bruttomesso and the police that would require the police to protect him. End of case.

## Freed Killer Butchers Two More... No Duty to Protect?

He was charged with murder in 1965, but Kahlil Ben Maatallah was never prosecuted because he was "incompetent to stand trial."[7] Instead, Clark County authorities placed him into the custody of various state

---

[6]The facts and law of this case are set forth in *Bruttomesso*, 591 P.2d 254.

[7]The facts and law of this case are set forth in *Whalen v. State of Nevada*, 679 P.2d 248 (Nev. 1984). *See also Whalen v. County of Clark*, 613 P.2d 407 (Nev. 1980).

agencies until December 1972. The prosecutors dropped the charges against Maatallah, but the court found him to be "both dangerous and insane" and committed him to the Las Vegas Mental Health Center. In July 1973, Maatallah was conditionally released; in July 1976, he was discharged from the mental hospital.

Eleven months later, without any provocation, Maatallah killed and butchered two men. The victims' wives sued the county, the state and the mental hospital. The wives argued that Clark County had negligently failed to prosecute Maatallah for the 1965 murder and had negligently treated him and failed to prevent his release from the mental hospital. The trial court dismissed these claims and the Supreme Court affirmed those rulings. The Court held that the County could not be sued for failing to prosecute a murderer, and owed no duty to control Maatallah after his release.[8]

The wives' claims against the state and the mental hospital barely survived in the courts. Their claims hinged on a technicality. The state and the hospital were immune from being sued for their negligence if Maatallah was on "conditional release" when he killed the two men, but they could be liable if Maatallah were "discharged" at the time he killed them.[9]

What does all of this mean? Simply this: you usually won't be able to sue the state and local governments in Nevada for their failing to prosecute suspected murderers, and their failing to keep criminally insane

---

[8]*Whalen,* 613 P.2d at 408.

[9]*Whalen,* 679 P.2d at 249-250 & nn. 3-5, *quoting and applying* Nev. Rev. Stat. § 433A.380.

suspects off the streets. You can't depend upon the government to protect you from violent criminals even when the authorities know who the criminals are.

You would be better served to be armed and prepared to competently protect yourself against crime in Nevada... unless you care to spin the roulette wheel of justice *after* you have become a victim.

# State of New Hampshire

The rule about the duty owed by the police to protect citizens is a little different in New Hampshire. Like several other states, citizens can sue the government for damages,[1] except for cases where the governmental entity negligently performed or failed to perform a "discretionary executive or planning function or duty."[2]

The New Hampshire Supreme Court has interpreted the phrase "discretionary executive or planning function" as referring to when a government makes "a basic policy decision which is characterized by the exercise of a high degree of official judgment or discretion."[3] In other words, the governmental entity cannot be sued for conduct that involved "weighing alternatives and making choices [about] public policy and planning."[4]

Under New Hampshire law, the "public duty" rule does not apply.[5] Thus, in cases where a citizen sues the police department for failing to protect her, the trial courts have to decide in each case whether the citizen's

---

[1]N.H. Rev. Stat. Ann. § 541-B:1-10; *see also* § 99-D:1 (sovereign immunity for state and its officers).

[2]N.H. Rev. Stat. Ann. § 541-B:19(c).

[3]*Mahan v. New Hampshire Dept. Of Admin. Services*, 693 A.2d 79, 82 (N.H. 1997).

[4]*Id.*

[5]*Doucette v. Town of Bristol*, 635 A.2d 1387, 1390 (N.H. 1993) (interlocutory appeal to decide whether police owe a duty to protect a citizen against the criminal violence of another citizen).

"interests are entitled to legal protection against the [police department's] conduct."[6]

## Police Duty To Arrest Drunken Teenagers

Five teenagers pooled their money, in the evening of September 11, 1982, to buy a case of beer.[7] The teens drank the beer as they drove around the Town of Kingston in a car. After observing the car traveling about 65 miles per hour in a 40 mile per hour zone, the town police stopped the car at about 8:20 p.m. Upon approaching the car, one of the officers actually took a beer bottle out of the driver's hand and dumped out the beer. The police found that all of the teens had been drinking, and 10 beers out of the 24 in the case were missing. The driver had "glassy eyes." Yet the police did not conduct a field sobriety test. An officer told the driver that a report concerning the illegal transportation of alcoholic beverages would be sent to the department of motor vehicles, and the driver's license might be suspended. After confiscating the remaining beer, the police allowed the teens to drive away. The officers did not even contact any of the teens' parents.

The teens drove to Massachusetts and bought more beer and drank nearly an entire case among them. By midnight they were all drunk. While driving home, the teens saw headlights behind them. Thinking it was the police, the driver panicked and starting speeding,

[6]*Id.* at 1391.

[7]The facts and law of this case are set forth in *Weldy v. Town of Kingston,* 514 A.2d 1257 (N.H. 1986).

exceeding 100 miles per hour. Rounding a curve far too quickly, the car hit a cement marker and overturned. Three passengers suffered the most: one 16-year old girl was killed, a 13-year old girl was seriously injured, and another boy was also injured.

The injured persons sued the police for failing to carry out their duty on two grounds. First, a New Hampshire statute required police officers to confiscate any illegally transported alcoholic beverages and to arrest any person "in charge" of transporting those beverages.[8] The police had failed to obey that statute.

Second, the Town of Kingston had an "unwritten policy" not to detain teenagers who were found illegally transporting alcohol and not to necessarily notify their parents. By carrying out that policy and not stopping the drunken teens from driving that night, the police committed a "violation of the common law duty of care." The state Supreme Court held that "[p]olice officers are obligated to protect the general public, and reasonable prudence dictates that teenagers illegally transporting alcohol be detained."

It is quite conceivable that the police and the city would owe a common law duty to protect or rescue citizens who dial 911 in New Hampshire. To date, however, no court has declared that such a duty exists. Who volunteers to be the first person to test the law?

---

[8]N.H. Rev. Stat. Ann. § 180:2.

# State of New Jersey

In New Jersey, police officers have a duty to investigate reports of criminal behavior.[1] Yet the police cannot be held liable for failing to arrest a suspected criminal.[2] A city cannot be held liable for failing to enforce any law.[3] One statute comes right out and says it: "Neither a public entity nor a public employee is liable for failure to provide police protection service, or, if [it] is provided, for failure to provide sufficient police protection service."[4]

Yet the law is rarely crystal clear. Consider these cases below.

## *Dangerous Man Outside Police Station... No Duty*

On February 9, 1974, the Berkeley Heights police were notified that, just a short distance from the police station, John Delia was menacing people with a shotgun.[5] The police did nothing. Less than 12 hours later, in the same vicinity, Delia willfully shot and killed John Wuethrich. Mrs. Wuethrich, on behalf of herself and her three children, sued the township for failing to take appropriate action to prevent Delia from harming her husband.

---

[1]*Wuetrich v. Delia*, 382 A.2d 929, 930 (N.J. App. 1978) (*per curiam*).

[2]N.J. Stat. Ann. § 59:5-5 (1992).

[3]N.J. Stat. Ann. § 59:2-4.

[4]N.J. Stat. Ann. § 59:5-4.

[5]The facts and law of this case are set forth in *Wuetrich v. Delia*, 341 A.2d 365 (N.J. Super. 1975).

In this case, the trial court refused to dismiss Mrs. Wuethrich's case before some evidence was gathered by both sides. The court ruled that "once clear warning of a threat to take life was received by the police, the police had a ministerial and operational duty to investigate." Whether the police were required to respond, and the way that they might have to respond, was still open to debate.[6]

The town was later able to provide evidence to sustain its claim of immunity from suit. The trial court dismissed the claim against the town, and the court of appeal affirmed. Ultimately, the police's duty to investigate does not mean that the police also have a duty to arrest a suspect or to protect others from that suspect's violence.[7]

When you dial 911, what exactly can you expect?

## *A Tale of Two Cases*

Figuring out what duties the police in New Jersey actually owe is not easy. Consider first the case in 1990 when police responded to Joanne Campbell's call that her estranged husband, Michael, was bothering her on her premises.[8] A court's restraining order was already in force which prohibited Michael from harassing or having any contact with Joanne or her family. The police knew about previous incidents when Michael had attacked Joanne at her home.

---

[6]*Id.* at 372.

[7]*Wuetrich v. Delia,* 382 A.2d at 930.

[8]The facts and law of this first case are set forth in *Campbell v. Campbell,* 682 A.2d 272 (N.J. Super. 1996).

The police ordered Michael off the property, and he left. A short time after the police left Joanne's home, Michael returned and shot Joanne. Joanne sued the police for failing to enforce the New Jersey Prevention of Domestic Violence Act[9] and protect her.

The trial court found that the police owed a duty to enforce that Act because of the special circumstances of this case (restraining order, knowledge of previous attacks). These circumstances made the police's duty to protect Joanne not a "discretionary duty"— the police were required to protect her under the Act. The other New Jersey statutes that immunized the police did not apply here. When the police failed to adequately perform that duty, they could be sued.

In the second case, in 1985, a young engaged couple were having a cookout.[10] Robert Morgan was invited, had a few beers, left, and then returned with several uninvited guests. Morgan's nephew spoke up to chide Morgan for bringing people who were not invited. Morgan pulled a knife and threatened to kill his nephew. The host of the party grabbed Morgan until he calmed down and then told Morgan to leave. Morgan left, but said he would return and kill both his nephew and the host.

The host called the Camden police, and two officers came to the house, but left just a few minutes later. Only a short time had passed when Morgan returned with a shotgun. The host's fiancee called the police again, and Morgan ran away. When the police arrived,

---

[9]N.J. Stat. Ann. §§ 2C:25-17 - 25-33.

[10]The facts and law of this second case are set forth in *Lee v. Doe*, 557 A.2d 1045 (N.J. App. 1989).

the host told them about the shotgun, and asked them to stay and patrol the area. The police refused, and told him not to worry.

Just after the police left, Morgan came back and tried to get in through the front door. He managed to jam his shotgun into the doorway crack as the door was slammed against him. Morgan fired the shotgun and severely injured the host.

The trial court and the state court appeals agreed: the police could not be sued for failing to protect the host from Morgan's violence. The police had never promised to give protection, and the police's actions did not increase the risk of harm. Accordingly, the New Jersey police immunity statutes applied with full force.

In the first case, because of a domestic violence law, Joanne Campbell got the right to sue... after she was severely injured. In the second case, the young couple learned the hard way: dialing 911 provides no guarantee of police protection in New Jersey.

Now that you've seen how the law works, would you bet your life on 911 service?

# State of New Mexico

The legislature of New Mexico made it possible under some circumstances to sue police departments for negligently failing to protect victims of crime.[1] The state Supreme Court has interpreted that law to allow the lawsuits.[2] To win such a suit, the victim's attorney must prove that the police department owed a duty to protect the victim, and that by breaching that duty, the police caused the victim to be harmed.[3]

So, in one case the police did not respond to a call reporting a crime in progress and requesting assistance. Because the police did not respond, the victim suffered a brutal rape and torture.[4] The New Mexico Supreme Court allowed the suit to go forward against the police.

A 1985 decision came to a similar result.[5] A bar had served alcohol to a patron who was already drunk. Later that night sheriff deputies saw the patron fire several gun shots outside of the bar. The deputies did nothing to stop or arrest the patron. A little while later, the patron got into his car and drove onto the highway. Not far away, the drunk patron crossed the center line and crashed head on into a car carrying a family on vacation, killing three of the four family members.

The New Mexico Supreme Court held that the police department could be sued for negligence. There were

---

[1] Tort Claims Act, New Mex. Stat. Ann. § § 41-4-1 to 41-4-29.

[2] *Schear v. County of Bernalillo*, 687 P.2d 728 (N.M. 1984).

[3] *Id.* at 730.

[4] *Id.* at 729.

[5] The facts and law are set forth in *California First Bank v. State of New Mexico*, 801 P.2d 646 (N.M. 1990).

allegations that the police had a policy *not* to interfere with patrons at certain bars, and not to arrest persons driving under the influence of alcohol. The police had also failed to stop this particular patron when they should have realized that he posed a risk of harm to others. State laws that immunized police from some suits would not shield them from liability in this case.

New Mexico's law does not allow all suits against law enforcement authorities, however. Two criminals, each a psychotic with a documented history of violence, escaped from a minimum security New Mexico prison.[6] Left unguarded at night in a facility without proper surveillance lighting, protective fencing or proper supervision, the two convicts escaped at 4:10 a.m. on March 1, 1982.

The New Mexico state police knew of the escape within two hours and notified all state and local authorities, but did not inform Colorado authorities. The two escapees crossed the border, robbed a Colorado liquor store and killed an employee there.

The heirs of the employee sued the New Mexico authorities for failing to properly classify the vicious convicts, failing to prevent their escape, and failing to notify Colorado authorities of their escape. New Mexico laws required the authorities to properly keep prisoners in custody, to correctly classify prisoners for security, and to cooperate with neighboring state police forces. Those laws didn't matter in this case. The New Mexico court of appeals held that the heirs could not sue the prison authorities because neither the prison

---

[6]The facts and law are set forth in *Wittkowski v. State of New Mexico*, 710 P.2d 93 (N.M. App. 1985).

nor its officials fell under any law that allowed them to be sued. As a result, all of the state entities and employees were immune from suit.

New Mexico belongs to the "Die Now, Sue Later" category. The police owe citizens a duty to protect them, under certain conditions. After you are dead, your heirs can sue for damages, at their own expense. Maybe they will win, and maybe they will lose. Comforting, isn't it?

# State of New York

The courts of New York have long held that a city government has no duty[1] to provide police protection to any particular person, unless there is a "special relationship" that creates such a "special duty" in a specific case.[2] In a few cases the courts have found a "special duty" where "a municipality's voluntary undertaking has lulled the injured party into a *false sense of security* and has thereby *induced him to relax his own vigilance or to forego other available avenues of protection.*"[3]

Two actual "dial 911" cases dramatically show how giving up the power to defend oneself and depending on the local police can be fatal. A third case unforgettably recalls a young woman's tragic fate when the law first disarmed her, then refused to protect her, and later denied liability for its actions.

## *Sorry, Victim Must Dial 911 Herself*

Screams came from Apartment 7A just after midnight on June 3, 1982, and a neighboring tenant saw a man with a gun near that apartment.[4] The neighbor called the New York City police by dialing 911. The police were dispatched; officers arrived

---

[1]See the discussion of "duty" in the chapter entitled "Brief Summary of the Law."

[2]*See e.g. Riss v. City of New York*, 240 N.E.2d 860 (N.Y. 1967).

[3]*Cuffy v. City of New York*, 505 N.E.2d 937 (N.Y. 1987) (italics added; holding city not liable, and reversing $1.3 million award for victims).

[4]The facts of this case are set forth in *Merced v. City of New York*, 534 N.Y.S.2d 60 (N.Y. Sup. Ct. 1987) (trial court decision).

shortly and buzzed Apartment 7A to be let in. There was no response.

The officers returned to the patrol car, and radioed for the 911 dispatcher to call the neighbor back so that she could "buzz in" the policemen. Shortly later the officers were "buzzed in" to the lobby where a different tenant told them "that everything was quiet and that it was probably just a family dispute." The officers left without visiting the seventh floor apartment or checking any further.

Minutes later, the 911 dispatcher received another call from a neighboring tenant stating that the police had not responded and help was needed. The dispatcher contacted the same officers. The officers reported "all was well and under control." The officers did not return to the building.

Neighbors found the tenant of Apartment 7A the next day. Twenty-two years old and the mother of an infant, Mrs. Merced had bled to death of a gunshot wound.

The estate of Mrs. Merced sued the city for negligently failing to protect Mrs. Merced after the 911 calls. Five years later, a New York trial court awarded her heirs $584,000. Another three years later, the New York Court of Appeals, the state's highest court, reversed the award and dismissed the case.[5]

Mrs. Merced's estate could not obtain damages from the police department, the Court said, for two reasons. First, Mrs. Merced herself had not personally contacted the police. Her neighbors had heard her screams and

---

[5]The controlling legal analysis for this case is set forth in *Merced v. City of New York*, 551 N.E.2d 589 (N.Y. 1990).

dialed 911— Mrs. Merced had not talked to the police herself.

Second, because Mrs. Merced had not personally dialed 911, she never received any promise that the police would help her. It did not matter that her neighbors had made the calls. Since she received no promise of help, Mrs. Merced could not have "justifiably relied" on the police. Mrs. Merced had no personal contact with the police, no promise of help, and no justifiable reliance. The legal requirements under New York law were not met.

Mrs. Merced's neighbors dialed 911... and Mrs. Merced died.

## *We Won... but Mom is Still Dead*

A burglar invaded the Kenmore, New York, home of Mrs. Amalia De Long on October 25, 1976.[6] At 9:29 a.m., just as the burglar was breaking in, Mrs. De Long dialed 911, reported hearing and seeing the burglar, and gave her address as 319 Victoria.

Two mistakes cost Mrs. De Long her life. The dispatcher mistakenly wrote the address as 219 Victoria. Because he knew there was a Victoria Avenue in Buffalo, he assumed that the address was in Buffalo instead of Kenmore. Buffalo and Kenmore were served by the same 911 system and the same dispatchers, but not the same police departments.

Buffalo police officers responded to the urgent dispatch of "burglary in progress," and within three minutes reported that the 219 Victoria Avenue address

---

[6]The facts and law of this case are set forth in *De Long v. County of Erie*, 457 N.E.2d 717 (N.Y. 1983).

did not exist *in Buffalo*. The dispatcher cleared the call and took no further action.

*Mrs. De Long's home on 319 Victoria Avenue was just 1,300 feet from the Kenmore Police Department.*

At about 9:42 a.m., witnesses saw Mrs. DeLong running from her home, naked and bleeding. She collapsed and a neighbor called the Kenmore police. Offices responded to that call within one minute, and paramedics arrived a few minutes later. By 9:53 a.m., Mrs. De Long, young wife and mother of three small children, was dead of multiple stab wounds.

Seven years later, Mrs. De Long's heirs eventually won their suit against Erie County. The New York Court of Appeals found that the police department did owe a special legal duty to protect Mrs. De Long.

First, Mrs. De Long had contacted the police personally.

Second, the evidence showed that the police had "promised" to give Mrs. De Long assistance. Erie County had encouraged the public to dial 911 instead of calling their local police departments, saying that it was more efficient that normal police services. Mrs. DeLong thus called the "more efficient" 911 service instead of the police department just a block away. The 911 dispatcher also had told her that police would be there "right away."

Third, Mrs. De Long justifiably relied on the promises that 911 was more efficient and that police would be arrive "right away." Because she relied on the 911 service, Mrs. De Long did not take other actions to protect herself until after she had been stabbed.

The evidence met the legal requirements, so her widowed husband and motherless children received money from the county government after a 7-year legal battle. Mrs. De Long dialed 911 and died.

## Police Won't Protect Unarmed Victim... No Duty

An ex-boyfriend with a criminal record was terrorizing Linda Riss.[7] He repeatedly threatened her, over a period of months in 1959, saying "If I can't have you, no one else will have you, and when I get through with you, no one else will want you." Linda called the New York City Police repeatedly to get protection, but she got none.

On one fateful day the ex-boyfriend let Linda know that the threatened attack was imminent. She called the police and urgently begged them for help—the police refused. The next day a hired thug threw lye into Linda's face, blinding her in one eye and permanently scarring her face.

Linda sued the city for failing to protect her. Nearly nine years after the police refused to protect Linda from the vicious attack, the New York Court of Appeals ruled that she had no right to police protection. Therefore, she could not sue the city for her grievous damages.

Judge Keating on the Court dissented from the ruling, pointing out that the same city that forbade Linda to have a weapon for self defense had also refused to protect her from criminal attack. In his dissenting opinion he wrote:

---

[7]The facts and law of this case are set forth in *Riss v. City of New York*, 240 N.E.2d 860 (N.Y. 1967).

What makes the city's position particularly difficult to understand is that, in conformity to the dictates of the law, Linda did not carry any weapon for self-defense. Thus, by a rather bitter irony she was required to rely for protection on the City of New York, which now denies all responsibility to her.

A bitter irony indeed.

# State of North Carolina

The "public duty doctrine" is alive and well in North Carolina. Under that common law doctrine, "a municipality and its agents act for the benefit of the public, and therefore, there is no liability for the failure to furnish police protection to specific individuals."[1] The North Carolina Supreme Court recognized "the limited resources of law enforcement personnel" and so the Court "refused to judicially impose liability for their failure to prevent every criminal act."[2]

There exist two exceptions to the no-liability rule. The first exception applies when "there is a special relationship between the injured party and the police."[3] For example, if a state's witness or informant has helped the police enforce the law, then the "special relationship" would exist.[4]

The second exception applies when the city or county creates a "special duty" to an individual. If the city police officers promised to protect an individual but fail to do so, and the individual suffered injury because he or she relied on officers' promise, then a "special duty" exists.[5]

How does North Carolina's law apply in practice?

---

[1]*Clark v. Red Bird Cab Company*, 442 S.E.2d 75, 77 (N.C. App. 1994), quoting the North Carolina Supreme Court's decision in *Braswell v. Braswell*, 410 S.E.2d 897, 901 (N.C. 1991).

[2]*Clark*, 442 S.E.2d at 77.

[3]*Braswell*, 410 S.E.2d at 902.

[4]*Id.*

[5]*Id.*, citing *Coleman v. Cooper*, 366 S.E.2d 2, 6 (N.C. App. 1988).

## *Armed & Crazy? Next Window, Please!*

Michael Hayes proved, on July 15, 1988, that he was dangerously crazy. Answering a dispatched call, a Forsyth County deputy sheriff visited Hayes in his moped shop. Hayes told the deputy that he planned to mount a shotgun on a moped and shoot the tires out of any car that "tried to run him off the road."[6] The deputy did nothing to stop Hayes.

The next day Hayes' mother called the Forsyth County Sheriff's Department and told them Hayes was crazy, needed to be committed to a mental hospital, and had a shotgun. Sheriffs' deputies visited Hayes again in his shop. Hayes arrogantly cursed the deputies and taunted them saying, "Come on back I have something for you." The deputies did not check Hayes' criminal record then. If they had checked, they would have discovered the outstanding warrant that would have empowered them to arrest Hayes immediately.

That same day, Hayes' grandfather, Garris Edwards, saw Hayes become so angry that he smashed both fists against a wall and broke one hand. Edwards took Hayes to the hospital, and then told a deputy sheriff about the situation and asked about having Hayes committed. The deputy told Edwards that Hayes could not be involuntarily committed at that time or in that county. The deputy was fatally wrong.

At 7:45 p.m. that night the Sheriff's Department received a call that Hayes "was having a nervous breakdown" and had a shotgun. At 7:50 p.m. Hayes' uncle called and reported Hayes was threatening to kill

---

[6]The facts and law of this case are set forth in *Hull v. Oldham,* 407 S.E.2d 611 (N.C. App. 1991).

his grandfather. At 7:55 p.m. the Department dispatched three deputies to the Hayes moped shop. The deputies were told to use caution because Hayes had a gun. When the deputies arrived near the shop they saw Hayes on his porch. The deputies did not even approach or talk to Hayes, but instead they stationed themselves at the local fire department location.

July 17, the next day, was the day of death. At 4:00 a.m. Hayes' grandfather (Edwards) called the Sheriff's Department again, and this time was told that Hayes could be involuntarily committed. The process would take about 8 hours, he was told, and would probably have to be done in the adjacent county where Hayes actually lived.

Edwards called the sheriffs again at 11:40 a.m. to report that Hayes was having a "nervous breakdown" and had threatened to kill him. Edwards begged for authorities to commit Hayes to a mental institution. He was told, in effect, that it was too much trouble that day and he should try to do it "tomorrow" in another county. Hayes' family members and friends called Forsyth County sheriffs five times trying to get help before the shooting started, to no avail.

Shortly later, police authorities received the calls: Hayes had begun his shooting spree. At 11:15 a.m. nearby Davidson County sheriffs learned Hayes had shot at a man in a pickup truck. The Davidson County deputy investigated the damage to the truck, but ignored the ongoing shooting down the street.

At 11:24 a.m. Winston-Salem police learned that Hayes was shooting at passing cars. The police notified the sheriffs of this report. Edwards also called to report another person shot in a parking lot and that Hayes was going to kill more people. Hayes then killed a woman in another passing car. In the next few minutes, calls and reports flooded in about deaths and injuries caused by Hayes.

Finally, at 11:41 a.m., the first Forsyth County deputy arrived on the scene with several others following. Because the deputies had hastily blockaded a certain road, a family driving home through the area had to take an alternate road... which led them right into Hayes' killing zone. There were no lights or signs or warnings to prevent the family from taking that detour. The father was killed; the mother injured.

Just before noon, deputies shot and then arrested Hayes.

## No Duty, Just Insurance

Could the injured citizens and the heirs of the dead sue the sheriffs, the county or the city government for negligence? Could the victims get compensation for their damages? The short answer is "mostly no."

The North Carolina appeals court ruled that the police and the government owed no special duty to the individual citizens harmed. The sheriffs had no duty to give accurate advice about commitment procedures. The sheriffs had not promised to protect anyone in particular. The deputies' failure to check Hayes' criminal record did not matter, because they had no special legal duty to do so.

Only one part of the victims' claims against the government and sheriffs did survive. North Carolina law required sheriffs to have a professional negligence bond.[7] The bond is a type of insurance policy that will pay a person who is injured by the sheriff's "neglect, misconduct or misbehavior." The injured parties and heirs could sue the individual deputies to get the money from their professional negligence bonds. These bonds, of course, can only pay certain maximum amounts which would have to be divided up among all the victims. And the victims would have to pay their own attorneys' fees and costs.

Before you dial 911 in North Carolina, perhaps you should first make sure that the sheriff's bond is in full force... and has enough value to protect your family from financial ruin after you are dead.

---

[7]*Id., citing* N. C. Gen. Statute § 162-8 (bond requirement) and § 58-76-5 (allowing suit on bond).

# State of North Dakota

Two statutes in North Dakota allow citizens to sue governmental entities.[1] The same statutes relieve the governmental entities from liability when they negligently perform (or fail to perform) their "discretionary functions."[2] The statutes also limit the city government's liability for damages to $250,000 per person and $500,000 total for the entire incident.[3] State liability is limited to $250,000 per person and $1,000,000 for the incident.[4]

The police cannot be sued for performing "discretionary functions." Not all of a police officer's activities are "discretionary functions," however. For example, when arresting a suspect the officer's duty to observe whether the suspect is drunk is discretionary. The officer's determination that the suspect is drunk is discretionary. Yet the officer's duty to inform the suspect's wife or family that the suspect had been arrested is *not* discretionary. Thus, an officer who fails to inform a suspect's family of his arrest for intoxication can incur liability for the suspect's damages.[5]

Will North Dakota courts impose a duty on the police department and the city to respond adequately

---

[1] N.D. Cent. Code § 32-12.1-03 (1) (political subdivisions); § 32-12.2-02(1)(state).

[2] N.D. Cent. Code § 32-12.1-03(3), § 32-12.2-02(3).

[3] N.D. Cent. Code § 32-12.1-03(2).

[4] N.D. Cent. Code §§ 32-12.2-02(2) .

[5] *McCroskey v. Fettes*, 310 N.W.2d 773, 775 (N.D. 1981).

to a 911 call? Do you want to be the first person to find out?

# State of Ohio

The Supreme Court of Ohio borrowed the common law rule of New York to hold that a city owes a duty to provide police protection to the public at large, but not to any particular individual.[1] The exception to the rule occurs when there is a "special relationship" between the city and the citizen involved.[2] Such a "special relationship" would exist if evidence shows the following four conditions:

(1) By its promises or actions, the city (through its police department) assumed the duty to act on behalf of the citizen;

(2) The police knew that inaction could lead to the citizen's harm;

(3) There was some form of direct contact between the police and the citizen before the harm; and

(4) the citizen justifiably relied on the police to do some specific act (as promised or indicated by the police).[3]

How does the Ohio law work in a real life and death situation?

---

[1] *Sawicki v. Village of Ottawa Hills*, 525 N.E.2d 468, 477-78 (Ohio 1988), following and applying *Cuffy v. City of New York*, 505 N.E.2d 937, 940 (N.Y. 1987).

[2] *Sawicki*, 525 N.E.2d at 478.

[3] *Id.*

## Police Station 300 Yards Away—
## No Duty

It was near midnight on September 17, 1981.[4] Todd Sabo and Leslie Sawicki were sitting in a van parked in a lot on the grounds of the apartment complex owned by her father, Peter Sawicki. The parking lot was located in the city of Toledo, but it was only about *300 yards away from the police station* for the village of Ottawa Hills.

Suddenly, Anthony Cook accosted Todd and Leslie and demanded their money at gunpoint. Cook ordered Leslie to tie up Todd with a wire, and then he himself bound Todd's legs. Cook then tied Leslie's hands behind her back, and stripped her of her clothes and prepared to rape her. While Cook was loosening his own clothes, Leslie pulled free her hands and attacked Cook. Todd also freed himself, joined the attack, and got control of Cook's gun.

While Todd sat on Cook's stomach with the gun pointed between Cook's eyes, Leslie escaped from the van. She ran partially nude to the apartment complex and telephoned the Ottawa Hills Police Department. Leslie informed the Ottawa Hills dispatcher of the address, that the attacker had a gun, and that the attacker had attempted to rape her. She asked the dispatcher to send help and he said, "Okay."

Within a minute the dispatcher reported a rape in progress to the Toledo Police Department, gave the wrong address, and almost no other information. The police responded Code 2 (high priority). Meanwhile,

---

[4]The facts and law of this case are set forth in *Sawicki v. Village of Ottawa Hills*, 525 N.E.2d 468 (Ohio 1988).

Leslie telephoned her father, Peter, who responded immediately in his bare feet and pajamas. Immediately afterward Leslie's mother called the Toledo police to report the situation in detail. When correctly apprised of the facts, the Toledo police upgraded their response to Code 3 (lights and siren).

At the same time, Leslie called the Ottawa Hills police again and gave a more detailed report. The dispatcher told Leslie that Ottawa Hills would not respond, but that Toledo police should be on their way. The dispatcher then called Toledo police again and gave an accurate and more detailed report.

## *Rash Decision Turned Lethal*

Peter Sawicki arrived on the scene quickly and found Todd holding Cook at gunpoint. Peter told Todd to bring Cook out of the van. Holding a gun to Cook's head, Todd brought him out and sat on him again. About two minutes later, after Peter and Leslie had kicked and hit Cook, Todd tossed away the firearm. The gun was a short distance away, but not entirely out of reach.

Cook grabbed control of the gun and shot Todd in the head and neck, and shot Peter in the neck. As Cook was escaping in a nearby parked car, the Toledo police arrived.

The total time from the first call to Toledo police and their arrival on scene was just under seven minutes. The police arrived just seconds after Cook had shot his two victims. The seconds lost because of the dispatcher's errors cost a life.

Todd eventually recovered from his injuries. Peter died in the hospital. Cook was convicted of various crimes including the murder of Peter Sawicki.

## No Police Liability

Could Leslie and her mother sue Ottawa Hills police for failing to respond to the emergency call, and for the dispatcher's failure to give the right information to the Toledo police in the first call? The judicial answer was "no," for several reasons.

First, Ohio law and local police regulations deprived police officers of the power to arrest anyone outside of the boundaries of their formal jurisdiction.[5] An officer who acted outside of his or her jurisdiction would even lose insurance coverage.[6] Ottawa Hills officers knew these rules and limitations quite well. Therefore, the Ottawa Hills officers not only had no duty to respond to Leslie's distress calls, they were forbidden to respond.

Second, the dispatcher had not assumed any duty for the Ottawa Hills police to respond. He had only said that he would send help. The dispatcher, by contacting Toledo police, had "sent help." The dispatcher made no promises of help to Leslie.

Third, Peter Sawicki had never talked to the Ottawa Hills dispatcher. Therefore, he had no direct contact with the dispatcher and could not have expressly relied on the dispatcher's promise to send help.

---

[5] *Sawicki,* 525 N.E.2d at 473, *citing* Ohio. Rev. Code § 2935.03 (and noting narrow exceptions such as for "hot pursuit").

[6] *Sawicki,* 525 N.E.2d at 473, *citing* Ohio Rev. Code § 737.04 and § 737.10.

The Ohio Supreme Court held that there was no legal "special relationship" that would place a duty on the Ottawa Hills police to protect Leslie, Peter or Todd. Merely calling the police does not create such a duty. Regardless of what the dispatcher says during the call, no special duty arises to require the police to protect the caller.

Even if you are 300 yards away from the police station, you cannot depend upon police to respond to your 911 call. You might be just over the line of jurisdiction. And giving up your gun, expecting the police to arrive any second, can be deadly.

# State of Oklahoma

The Oklahoma legislature adopted statutes that hold the state and municipal governments immune from tort lawsuits, with certain specific exceptions.[1] One statute, however, expressly provides that governmental entities cannot be held liable for negligently performing or failing to perform "discretionary" acts.[2] The law is even more specific: the government cannot be sued for negligently failing to provide police, law enforcement, or fire protection, or for failing to prevent or quell riots.[3]

Under Oklahoma law, do the police owe a duty to provide adequate police protection to members of the public, such as by responding to 911 calls? They probably do not owe such a duty. For example, in one case a local fire department negligently failed to maintain the fire hydrant serving one neighborhood and failed to have any backup in case the hydrant did not function properly.[4] Because of the delays in getting enough water, the fire fighters were unable to prevent a house from being destroyed by fire. The Oklahoma Supreme Court held that the homeowners could not sue the fire department because the statute precluded suits against government for failure to provide fire protection.

---

[1]Okla. Stat. Ann. tit. 51, § 152.1.

[2]Okla. Stat. Ann. tit. 51, § 155(5).

[3]Okla. Stat. Ann. tit. 51, § 155(6)

[4]The facts and law of this case are set forth in *Shockey v. City of Oklahoma City*, 632 P.2d 406 (Okla. 1981).

Applying the same statute to another case, the state Supreme Court held that a person injured while in protective custody could not sue the county police.[5] In that case, the deputy had taken the person into protective custody and placed the person into the patrol car. The person had jumped from the car, or fallen out of the car, and suffered injuries. Although it was quite possible that the deputy had not acted negligently, the Oklahoma Court *would not even permit the case to go to trial so that a jury could decide*. The Court held that such a lawsuit would put the police department's method of providing police protection on trial, and that was what the statute prohibited.

If the police owe no legal duty to protect your home from fire, and no duty to protect you when you are in their "protective custody," then will they owe you a duty to respond adequately to your 911 emergency call?

---

[5]The facts and law of this case are set forth in *Schmidt v. Grady County*, 943 P.2d 595 (Okla. 1997).

# State of Oregon

Uncertain, unpredictable, baffling. These words describe Oregon's law concerning the duty of the police towards citizens. The Oregon Tort Claims Act holds governmental entities liable for torts they commit, with several exceptions.[1] Governmental entities cannot be held liable for negligently performing or failing to perform discretionary functions or duties.[2] They also cannot be held liable for damages arising from a riot or mob action, or because of any action they take (or fail to take) to prevent riots or mob actions.[3]

It is difficult to know exactly how the rules will work in a situation when a citizen dials 911 to get protection from a violent criminal attack. Consider the following cases:

◆  ◆  ◆

Robert Cook was attacked while on campus watching a girls' high school basketball game.[4] According to the court, the school did owe a duty to take precautions to protect people from the "reasonably foreseeable acts of third parties." But there was not enough evidence to show that the school knew or should have known that there was a substantial risk of violence against Cook. Case dismissed.

---

[1] Or. Rev. Stat. Ann. § 30.265.

[2] Or. Rev. Stat. Ann. § 30.265(3)(c).

[3] Or. Rev. Stat. Ann. § 30.265(3)(e).

[4] The facts and law of this case are set forth in *Cook v. School District UH3J*, 731 P.2d 443 (Or. App. 1987).

Henrietta Nearing separated from her husband and was living with their two very young children in April 1980, when the husband came into the home and hit Henrietta.[5] Henrietta reported the incident to the police who then arrested the husband. The husband was charged with assault, and the court issued a restraining order which forbade him from bothering Henrietta or entering her home. About a month later, the husband entered Henrietta's home, broke up the place, and tried to take the two children. Henrietta reported these actions to the police, but the officer refused to arrest the husband because the officer did not actually see the husband commit a crime on her property.

The husband returned on other occasions to attack Henrietta, her friend, and her property. He threatened to kill Henrietta's friend several times. The police did not enforce the restraining order by arresting the husband. After Henrietta sued, the court held that the police did owe a duty to enforce the restraining order, particularly because a special domestic violence law required police to make arrests in these sorts of situations. The officer and the governmental entities were not immune from suit. Whether a jury would decide in favor of Henrietta was a matter for another day.

◆  ◆  ◆

With a Marion County police officer speeding after him, a fleeing criminal crashed his car into an innocent driver's car.[6] The innocent driver suffered injuries in

---

[5]The facts and law of this case are set forth in *Nearing v. Weaver*, 670 P.2d 137 (Or. 1983).

[6]The facts and law of this case are set forth in *Lowrimore v.*

the wreck and sued the policeman and the city, charging that the officer had negligently driven his police car at an unreasonably high speed during the chase. The Oregon Supreme Court held that the police cannot be sued for negligently performing a "discretionary function." But a "discretionary function" is one that involves making a "policy judgment." The decision to chase a car was not a "policy judgment," and therefore the police could be sued for negligently conducting the chase. A jury would ultimately decide the question.

◆ ◆ ◆

A friend brought Marilyn Scovill to the police station.[7] Scovill, who had a history of trouble with the police, was visibly drunk and disoriented, and she was unable to care for herself. The police said they would take care of Scovill, perhaps place her in a detox center, so the friend left. On her person the police found three butcher knives, and confiscated them. Then the police allowed Scovill to leave the police station. She walked out into traffic and was killed.

The Oregon Supreme Court held that because a state statute required it, the police owed a duty to take the obviously intoxicated Scovill to a treatment facility. As the police failed to obey the statute, Scovill's estate could sue the police for damages. Oregon's government immunity laws did not preclude a lawsuit, so a jury would decide whether the police had been negligent.

◆ ◆ ◆

---

*Dimmitt*, 797 P.2d 1027 (Or. 1990).

[7]The facts and law of this case are set forth in *Scovill v. City of Astoria*, 921 P.2d 1312 (Or. 1996).

Ms. Mosley, a high school student, was cut by another student wielding a knife in a fight during lunch period.[8] She sued the school for negligently failing to properly supervise the students, failing to provide proper security when the school knew that some students carried weapons in school, failing to prevent students from bringing weapons to school, and failing to stop the fight before the knife was used.

A jury heard the case, and found the defendant school district not liable. The Oregon appeals court held that the school district should not even have been sued for failing to provide proper security and for failing to prevent students from bringing weapons to school.[9] The school, being a governmental entity, cannot be held liable for its "policy decisions" about how much security to provide and how to provide it. The Oregon Supreme Court in turn held that the school could not be sued for failing to properly supervise the students, because that claim also involved the school's policy decision about how to provide security. The high court also held that there was so little evidence that the school was negligent that the case should have been dismissed before trial.

♦ ♦ ♦

Dwain Little sexually assaulted and murdered a young girl in 1964.[10] He was convicted of first degree murder and sentenced to life imprisonment. The State

---

[8]The facts and law of this case are set forth in *Mosley v. Portland School District No. 1J*, 843 P.2d 415 (Or. 1992).

[9] *See Mosley v. Portland School District No. 1J*, 813 P.2d 71 (Or. App. 1991).

[10] The facts and law of this case are set forth in *Hendricks v. State of Oregon*, 678 P.2d 759 (Or. App. 1984).

Board of Parole granted him parole in July, 1974. Ten months later, Little violated his parole by committing a weapons violation and was returned to prison. The Board paroled him again in 1977. On June 2, 1980, Little kidnapped, raped and brutally stabbed Ann Hendricks. Fortunately, she did not die, and he was convicted of rape and assault.

Ms. Hendricks sued the Board of Parole for negligently releasing Little when they knew or should have known that he was a "dangerous psychotic with homicidal tendencies who had killed a least once in the past." She also charged that the Board was negligent in failing to properly treat Little's mental condition and in failing to properly consider the warnings given by state police about Little.

The Oregon appeals court held that the Board's decisions to release Little on parole in 1974 and 1977 could not be challenged by this lawsuit. The Board's decisions were "policy judgments." Governmental entities cannot be sued for exercising their "discretion" when making such judgments. Case dismissed.

♦ ♦ ♦

A convicted felon escaped from a work camp by stealing the state's van (which had its ignition keys left inside).[11] Two days later and 50 miles away, the escaped convict stole a gun from his mother's house and shot two people, killing one. The survivor and the estate of the dead victim sued the state prison system for negligently allowing the convict to escape, failing to

---

[11]The facts and law of this case are set forth in *Buchler v. Oregon Corrections Division*, 853 P.2d 798 (Or. 1993).

recapture the prisoner, and failing to warn the general public that he had escaped.

The Oregon Supreme Court held that the state prison system, under these circumstances, owed no tort duty to prevent the escape, capture the convict, or warn the public. The Court's decision rested mainly on the evidence that the prison authorities did not know that the convict was "likely to cause bodily harm to others if not controlled." That convict did not have a record of violent crime; he had been convicted of property crimes and burglary, and had a history of violent temper and drug problems. Case dismissed.

## Conclusion?

The variety of case decisions in Oregon makes it hard to know whether the state courts will hold that the police owe a duty to protect victims of crime who call 911. Oregon's Supreme Court has adopted the general rule that Person A has "no duty" to control the conduct of a Person C and prevent Person C from causing harming Person B (unless there is a "special relationship" between the Person A and Person B). Generally, there is no "special relationship" between the government and members of the general public.[12] Therefore, the government has no duty to protect members of the general public from criminal violence.

Of course, the decision about the law will occur after the criminal attack and after the victim is injured or killed without receiving adequate police protection. Would you prefer to rely on the court system after a

---

[12]*Buchler*, 853 P.2d at 801, *adopting* Restatement (Second) of Torts § 315 (1965).

criminal assault or invasion... or would you prefer to be prepared in advance to drive away anybody who comes looking for trouble?

# Commonwealth of Pennsylvania

Police in Pennsylvania "have no duty to provide protection to specific individuals."[1] A narrow exception to the no-duty rule applies when there exists a "special relationship" between the police and crime victim.[2] Even when the police owe a duty to protect a citizen because of a "special relationship," the law might immunize the police from liability for failing to carry out the duty.[3]

Under Pennsylvania statutes, the Commonwealth and local governments are immune from liability for negligence except where the legislature has provided otherwise.[4] On the other hand, a statute holds local governments liable for negligence, unless they are immune under the common law or another statute.[5]

Confusing? Consider the following cases to see how the Pennsylvania courts apply the law.

## *Gang Fight, Cops Called, Child Killed... No Duty*

A fight between two groups started on September 10, 1987, behind the Philadelphia home of Mae Vern Yates and her daughters Sylvia and Cynthia.[6] The

---

[1] *Johnson v. City of Philadelphia*, 657 A.2d 87, 89 (Pa. Commw. Ct. 1995).

[2] *Id.* at 89.

[3] *Id.*

[4] 42 Pa. Cons. Stat. Ann. § 8521 (state government), § 8541 (local government).

[5] 42 Pa. Cons. Stat. Ann. § 8542.

[6] The facts and law of this case are set forth in *Yates v. City of Philadelphia*, 578 A.2d 609 (Pa. Commw. 1990).

police came, talked to the two groups, and left. Shortly the fighting resumed, and Mrs. Yates heard someone shout, "He's got a gun." Mrs. Yates called the police and was told a police unit would be sent out.

Again, about a half hour later, Mrs. Yates heard someone shout, "He's got a gun." The police had not yet responded, so she called the police back. Two police cars arrived on the scene, but the officers did not even get out of their cars or disperse the crowd. A short while later both police vehicles left. When the police were gone, a shot was fired somewhere behind the Yates home where the fighting was. The bullet entered the home and killed young Sylvia.

Could the Yates family sue the City of Philadelphia for negligently failing to stop the fighting and protect the family from violent harm? The courts said "no."

Wrote the Pennsylvania Commonwealth Court: "The general rule of law is that municipalities have no duty to protect a specific individual from the criminal act of third parties."[7] Only if there is a "special relationship" between the crime victim and the police can there be a duty to protect. A "special relationship" arises only when:

(1) specific potential victims face the risk of criminal attack because they have "aided law enforcement as informers or witnesses," or

(2) the "police have expressly promised to protect specific individuals from precise harm."

Merely calling the police does not create the "special relationship." In fact, even when a 911 operator fails to

---

[7] *Id.* at 610.

process an emergency call, there is no "special relationship."[8]

In the Yates' case, Mrs. Yates did not tell the police that she or her family were specifically threatened by violence. No gunshots had been fired before the actually killing. The police never promised to provide protection to them, and the police never gave any assurances of safety. All the police promised was to "investigate the disturbance." On these facts, the court held that the police did not have a "special relationship" with the Yates family, and therefore owed no duty to protect them.

As the court said: "The police did not undertake an obligation to provide a greater degree of protection to the Yates family than to anyone else in the neighborhood."[9] Case dismissed.

## Gas Station Attacked, Police Delay Response... No Duty

Four attackers invaded a gas station on June 28, 1980.[10] They viciously beat the owner, Charles Morris. They struck and terrorized his wife Sandra as she tried to shield her unconscious husband from further injury. The policeman on duty, Officer Musser, knew about the attack but did not respond in time to prevent or reduce the injuries suffered the victims. It so happens that

---

[8] *Id.* at 611, *citing Steiner v. City of Pittsburgh*, 509 A.2d 1368 (Pa. Commonw. 1986) (city cannot be liable for negligence of 911 dispatcher).

[9] *Id.* at 612.

[10] The facts and law of this case are set forth in *Morris v. Musser*, 478 A.2d 937 (Pa. Commonw. 1984).

Officer Musser had refused to assist crime victims in jeopardy on a previous occasion, yet the police department had not removed him from his job.

The Pennsylvania court's ruling shows how the law works to shield governmental entities from liability. First, the city was immune from liability entirely, for both failing to fire Officer Musser before and for failing to protect the victims in this case. Second, the officer himself was not immune and could be sued.

Third, however, the officer did not owe any duty to protect the victims in this case. As the court said, a police officer's obligation is "to protect the citizenry"— a duty that he owes "to the public at large, and not a specific duty owing to particular persons." There was no "special relationship" that would impose a duty on the police, because the Morris's were not police informants and they had never been promised specific protection against the attack.

No duty to protect means no liability for negligence means no lawsuit for damages. When criminals invade, Pennsylvania citizens are on their own.

Would the four attackers have invaded the gas station had they even suspected that the Morris's were armed and trained to shoot?

# Commonwealth of Puerto Rico

Under the laws of Puerto Rico, a citizen can sue the government for damages arising out of the negligence of the government or its employees, up to a limit of $75,000 per individual claim and $150,000 per claimant.[1] On the other hand, citizens cannot sue for the government's negligence in enforcing the law[2] or in carrying out "a function of a discretional nature."[3]

Meanwhile, the statute which creates the "Puerto Rico Police" states that the police department has the "duty to protect persons and property, to maintain and keep the public order, to observe and secure the utmost protection of the civil rights of the citizens, to prevent, [and] discover and [prosecute] crime."[4]

Does the Puerto Rico Police agency owe a tort duty to protect individual citizens from criminal attack, and to respond timely to 911 calls for help? If the courts of Puerto Rico follow the general law of the United States, then police response will likely be deemed "a function of a discretional nature." In that case, under the Puerto Rico statute, a citizen could not sue the police for negligently performing that function. The Supreme Court of Puerto Rico has yet to rule on this issue.

## When the Police Cannot Be Trusted

The results in one tragic case, however, suggest that the courts will hold that the Puerto Rico police owe no

---

[1] P.R. Laws Ann. tit. 32, § 3077 (1990)

[2] P.R. Laws Ann. tit. 32, § 3081(a).

[3] P.R. Laws Ann. tit. 32, § 3081(b).

[4] P.R. Laws Ann. tit. 25, § 1003 (1979).

tort duty to protect citizens, even when the police are terribly negligent. From 1982 to 1991, Rafi Rodriguez had physically and emotionally abused his wife Flor Maria Soto.[5]

Flor had submitted to the frequent beatings because Rafi had threatened to kill her and other members of her family, she had nowhere to go, and she did not think the police would help her. As it happened, Rafi had done gardening and auto repair work for several of the local police officers and was on a friendly basis with them.

On April 17, 1991, Rafi beat up Flor again. He had many times threatened her that he would kill her if she reported his abuse to the police. Flor could not stand it anymore, so she secretly told the police about the history of abuse and Rafi's repeated threats. She then took her children to stay at her mother's house.

The police failed to process Flor's report under the domestic violence laws. More importantly, they violated their legal duty of maintaining confidentiality — they told Rafi about her report. Two days later, Rafi confronted Flor about the report, and she denied it. The next day, Rafi came to Flor's mother's house to pick up the children for an outing at the beach. After the outing, Rafi kept the children at the family home and refused to give them back to Flor.

The next day, at 8:00 p.m on Sunday, April 21, Flor knew the kids had to go to school the following Monday, so she went back to the family home to get them. As she stood on the lawn, Flor heard both

---

[5]The facts and law of this case are set forth in *Soto v. Flores,* 103 F.3d 1056 (1st Cir. 1997).

children tell Rafi that she had arrived. Eight-year-old Sally shouted, "Run, Mommy, please run!" Rafi then shot his son in the forehead. Rafi heard Sally say to her father, "Daddy, no, Daddy, no." Rafi then shot Sally through her mouth. Flor heard a third shot. Rafi had killed himself.[6]

Flor sued the police for violating her civil rights by negligently telling the Rafi about her report and then failing to inform her about it and failing to protect her and the children from his lethal reaction. The police had also failed to inform Flor about getting a protective order and the availability of a women's shelter, even though the law required the police to take affirmative action to protect victims of spousal abuse.

The federal courts dismissed Flor's lawsuit without a trial. They held that she had no federal constitutional right to police protection from crime or domestic violence. The testimony of several officers showed that the local police department typically did not enforce the domestic violence law, and at least one of the police officers involved was openly hostile to that law. Even so, the courts held that Flor was not denied her constitutional rights.

Tellingly, Flor (through her lawyer) had brought her case on U.S. Constitutional grounds only. She did not even try to sue the police using local Puerto Rico laws.[7] This tactical decision suggests that lawyers in Puerto Rico know there is no remedy under local law. They probably expect the courts to hold that the police

---

[6]*Id.* at 1061.
[7]*Id.* at 1058.

cannot be sued for failing to protect citizens from crime.

Puerto Rico's "gun control" laws heavily restrict private firearms ownership.[8] Those laws worked to assure that only the victims were unarmed and defenseless. The peace officers were unwilling to enforce the domestic violence law, and they actively helped the known violent criminal. Does dialing 911 to get police assistance in Puerto Rico make any sense?

---

[8]See 25 P.R. Laws Ann. tit. 25, §§ 411-454.

# State of Rhode Island

When the government owes a general duty to the entire public, Rhode Island courts will not allow private individuals to sue the government for damages caused by its employees' negligently failing to carry out that duty.[1] This rule is called the "public duty doctrine." In other words, when the government owes a duty to everybody, then it doesn't owe a duty to anybody in particular. The purpose of the doctrine "is to encourage the effective administration of governmental operations by removing the threat of potential litigation."[2]

If the police are in a "special relationship" with a private individual, however, then the individual can sue for damages.[3] Also, if the government or its agent negligently does some common action such as driving a car or running a business location, then a person injured by that negligence can sue.[4]

The Supreme Court of Rhode Island has applied this doctrine consistently.

## Sorry, Patrolman—Our Mistake... No Duty

Anthony Souza was tried and convicted for a murder he committed in 1964.[5] He was sentenced to life imprisonment but escaped from prison in 1972. Souza

---

[1] *Catone v. Medberry*, 555 A.2d 328, 330 (R.I. 1989)

[2] *Id.* at 333.

[3] *Id.* at 330-331.

[4] *Id.* at 334.

[5] The facts and law of this case are set forth in *Orzechowski v. State*, 485 A.2d 545 (R.I. 1984).

was recaptured and convicted of escaping from prison. Inside prison Souza regularly violated prison regulations. Nevertheless, after he had served only 10 years of his life sentence, the state parole board granted parole to this murderer and violent criminal in 1976.

Two months after he was paroled, Souza and an accomplice robbed a liquor store. Patrolman Orzechowski and another officer responded to the distress call. When the officers arrived on the scene and were struggling to arrest the robbers, Souza shot Patrolman Orzechowski in the stomach and permanently disabled him.

As it happens, the state parole board had violated state law when it granted parole to Souza. Souza should not have been released so early. Orzechowski sued the parole board and the state for having violated its state law duty and thus having committed negligence by releasing the vicious Souza to the world. The parole board's negligence gave Souza the opportunity to rob the store and to shoot the patrolman.

The Supreme Court of Rhode Island agreed with the trial court that dismissed Orzechowski's law suit. Even though the parole board violated the law, the Court said, Orzechowski was not a "foreseeable" specific victim of that unlawful action. The parole board owed its duty to protect the public, not Orzechowski in particular. Therefore, Orzechowski (and his health insurance company, if any) would bear the cost of the parole board's negligence.

## Cop Allows "Less Drunk" To Drive...
## No Duty

The state does not even owe a duty to protect its own police officers from criminal activity that the state's negligence unleashes. Do you suppose the state owes private individuals a higher duty?

In one case a police officer in a bar parking lot stopped three drunk patrons.[6] The officer told the patrons to pull over to the side and wait until they sobered up before they drove home. One of the patrons got out of the car and explained to the officer how he was not as drunk as the others and would be able to drive. The officer discovered that this patron did not possess a driver's license at that time. In fact the patron had no license at all. Nevertheless, the officer allowed the patron to drive . Later the drunks switched drivers, and the car crashed into a utility pole. The "less drunk" young man was totally paralyzed as a result.

Could the paralyzed man, who had not been driving at the time, sue the officer for failing to prevent him or the other drunks from driving? The state Supreme Court held that the police officer owed a duty to protect the public in general, but not to protect specifically the people in that car. Just because the officer took some responsibility by first ordering the drivers to sober up before driving, and then allowing an unlicensed drunk to drive the car, that did not create the "special relationship" necessary to create a legal duty to the drunks as individuals. The lawsuit was dismissed.

---

[6]The facts and law of this case are set forth in *Barratt v. Burlingham*, 492 A.2d 1219 (R.I. 1985).

When it comes to being a victim of crime in the Ocean State, consider yourself a guppy among the sharks. The Rhode Island courts take a strong position against allowing injured citizens to sue the government for failing to protect them.[7] Think about that attitude as you are deciding whether to defend yourself or to rely solely on dialing 911...

---

[7] *See Catone,* 555 A.2d at 331 (listing cases).

# State of South Carolina

Under South Carolina law, the state and municipal governments are immune generally from lawsuits,[1] but the legislature allows the governments to be sued for many torts.[2] Citizens cannot sue a governmental entity, however, for negligently performing or failing to perform any act or service which involves exercising "discretion."[3] In particular, a city cannot be held liable for negligently failing to provide police protection or to prevent or quell a riot.[4]

Also, the "public duty" rule holds that public officials are generally not liable to individuals for their negligence in performing public duties "because the duty is owed to the public at large rather than to anyone individually."[5] Even when a state statute prescribes the duties of a public official, that does not mean that the official owes a duty to individual members of the public.

Accordingly, a citizen cannot sue a city for failing to provide adequate fire protection (*e.g.* failing to inspect and maintain water mains and hydrants).[6] Similarly, a citizen cannot sue the government for failing to enforce the law generally, or failing to detect a driver's being drunk and stop him from getting back on the road.[7]

---

[1]S.C. Code Ann. § 15-78-20.

[2]S.C. Code Ann. § 15-78-40.

[3]S.C. Code Ann. § 15-78-60(5).

[4]S.C. Code Ann. § 15-78-60(6)

[5]*Wells v. City of Lynchburg*, 501 S.E.2d 746, 751-52 (S.C. App. 1998).

[6]*Id.* at 748.

[7]*Patel v. McIntyre*, 667 F. Supp. 1131 (D.S.C. 1987), *affirmed,*

As the law stands today, there is no reason to believe that police in South Carolina owe a duty to protect any specific individual from criminal attack or necessarily to respond to a 911 call. There is no specific controlling legal decision on 911 liability... care to risk your life by relying on 911 alone?

848 F.2d 185 (4th Cir. 1988).

# State of South Dakota

Governmental entities can be sued in South Dakota to the extent that they have insurance for the claim.[1] The "public duty" rule, however, further limits government liability for torts.

Under the public duty rule, "government owes a duty of protection to the public, not to particular persons or classes."[2] The state Supreme Court has justified this rule because of scarce resources:

> Furnishing public safety always involves allocating limited resources. Law enforcement entails more than simply reacting to violations; it encompasses the art of keeping the peace. Deploying finite resources to achieve these goals is a legislative and executive policy function.[3]

If the government had a legal duty to protect individuals, then individuals could sue when the government failed. The result, said the high court, would be to "render government administration chaotic and enfeebled." Lawsuits would cause courts to scrutinize the government's alleged negligence instead of the criminal acts which actually caused the harm.

The South Dakota Court expressed the simple legal truth that the duties of the government (including the

---

[1] S. D. Codified Laws § 21-32-16 (state), § 21-32A-1 (public entity).

[2] *Tipton v. Town of Tabor*, 567 N.W.2d 351, 356 (S.D. 1997).

[3] *Id.* at 356.

police) are owed to the public as a whole, but not to any specific individual:

> [M]any enactments and regulations are intended only for the purpose of securing to individuals the enjoyment of rights and privileges to which they are entitled as members of the public, rather than for the purpose of protecting any individual from harm.[4]

Sometimes a police department can owe a "special duty" to an individual or class. The courts will recognize a special duty if (1) the police actually knew of a "dangerous condition," (2) the victim has reasonably relied on the police's statements or conduct, (3) there is a written law that requires the police to do specific acts to protect a particular class of persons, and (4) the police failed to act reasonably to avoid increasing the victim's risk of harm.[5]

Unless you can point to a specific law that grants you personal police protection, it seems that the police in South Dakota owe no duty to protect you from criminal attack. Would you feel comfortable telling

---

[4]*Id., quoting* Restatement (Second) of Torts § 288 cmt. b (1965).

[5]*Id.* at 355, *citing Tipton v. Town of Tabor*, 538 N.W.2d 783, 787 (S.D. 1995).

your family to rely solely on dialing 911 in an emergency?

# State of Tennessee

Private citizens cannot sue the state government of Tennessee or its officials for money damages, unless the legislature authorizes such a suit.[1] As it happens, the legislature has authorized suits against governmental entities and their employees for negligently performing official duties.[2]

The state legislature has declared certain exceptions, however. First, there is the general rule that city and county governments cannot be sued for negligently exercising or discharging their "governmental" or "proprietary" functions.[3] Second, city and county governments cannot be sued for the negligent performance of "discretionary" functions,[4] and they cannot be sued for damages arising from failure to quell riots, mob violence, or civil disturbance.[5]

The Tennessee courts have consistently applied the no-duty rule. The state Supreme Court thus wrote:

> It is the settled law in this state that private citizens, as such, cannot maintain an action complaining of the wrongful acts of public officials unless such private citizens [claim] special interest or a special injury not common to the public generally.[6]

---

[1]Tenn. Code Ann. § 20-13-102(a); *Cashion v. Robertson*, 955 S.W.2d 60, 63 (Tenn. App. 1997).

[2]Tenn. Code Ann. § 20-20-205.

[3]Tenn. Code Ann. § 29-20-101 (law applies to political subdivisions); § 29-20-201 (immunity).

[4]Tenn. Code Ann. § 29-20-205(1).

[5]Tenn. Code Ann. § 29-20-205(7).

[6]*Ezell v. Cockrell*, 902 S.W.2d 394, 397 (Tenn. 1995), *citing*

The "special duty" exception to this no-duty rule arises if, for example, the police take affirmative action to protect the citizen and the citizen relies on that action.[7] That exception also operates when a statute specifically allows a victim to sue a public official for injuries resulting from failure to enforce certain laws.[8] Under either circumstance, the police have a duty to protect the citizen.

What happens when a citizen sues the police for failing to protect him?

## *Police Chief Goes Berserk... No Liability*

Ray Bobo, Jr. was lawfully driving his truck on the night of August 24, 1946, when the chief of police stopped him.[9] The chief, named Corb Barner, complained about the muffler on Bobo's truck. There was a brief discussion, nobody got angry, and the two men shook hands.

Then Chief Barner stepped back from the truck and said "I think I am going to shoot hell out of you anyway." Chief Barner shot Bobo in the chest with his .38 caliber police revolver. Bobo suffered painful, serious and permanent injuries, but survived.

---

and quoting *Bennett v. Stutts*, 521 S.W.2d 575, 576 (Tenn. 1975).

[7]*Id.* at 402.

[8]*Id.*

[9]The facts and law of this case are set forth in *Bobo v. City of Kenton*, 212 S.W.2d 363 (Tenn. 1948). In 1973, the Tennessee legislature first enacted the Tennessee Governmental Tort Liability Act which modified in several respects the law of municipal liability for torts.

Bobo sued the city for its police chief's unlawfully shooting him, because the city knew or should have known that Barner was dangerous and therefore unsuitable to remain as chief. It so happened that the city had received numerous complaints about Chief Barner in the three months before the shooting. These complaints had indicated that Chief Barner was mentally unstable and a dangerous man, and that he should not be retained as chief of police. One of the complaints came from Barner's own half-brother. The city had done nothing about these complaints.

The trial court dismissed Bobo's case. The Tennessee Supreme Court affirmed that decision because "the maintenance of a police force by a municipality is a governmental function and hence [the city] is not liable for torts committed by its peace officers." The city owed no duty to Ray Bobo not to employ a homicidal maniac as chief of police.

## Police Failed to Arrest Violent Criminal... No Duty

Farris G. Morris, Jr. was arrested on August 23, 1994, and charged with aggravated rape.[10] Enough evidence existed to support a grand jury proceeding against Morris. Morris was not kept in custody, however. On September 7, 1994, a warrant was issued for Morris's arrest on a charge of violating his probation from a 1992 drug sale conviction. Sheriff Woolfork of Madison County received the warrant that day.

---

[10]The facts and law of this case are set forth in *Hurd v. Woolfork*, 959 S.W.2d 578 (Tenn. App. 1997).

Morris's neighbors had informed the Sheriff's Department that he was threatening people in the neighborhood. The Sheriff's Department did not process the September 7 warrant until sometime after September 17.

September 17 would have been too late anyway. On that day Morris brutally beat and stabbed a young woman who was visiting next door in the duplex where Morris lived. In that same house that day Morris also shot a man in the head with a shotgun.

The survivors of the two victims sued the sheriff and the county for negligently failing to process and execute the arrest warrant. Had Morris been arrested within a few days of September 7 (when the arrest warrant was issued), he would not have been able to murder the two innocent victims.

The survivors' lawsuit was dismissed by the trial court before a jury ever heard the evidence. The state appeals court affirmed the ruling for two main reasons. First, the sheriff had never taken any action to protect those two victims from Morris's violence, and the victims had never relied on any protective action. Second, although a state law did require the sheriff to diligently execute arrest warrants, that law did not specifically allow a citizen to sue the sheriff for failing to obey that law. The duty to keep the peace is a duty the sheriff owed to the public, and not to any particular individual.

Can you depend upon the police to protect you from crime in Tennessee? What is your best defense against criminal violent attack—dialing 911?

# State of Texas

Under the Texas Tort Claims Act, a city government is liable for damages arising from its government functions, including police and fire protection.[1] On the other hand, the law also states that there can be no liability for emergency response or failure to provide police or fire protection.[2] Texas law regarding emergency response liability is complicated, and it appears that a city will not be liable for negligently responding to a 911 call unless the city has violated a written law concerning 911 calls.[3]

The government entity has no enforceable duty to respond to a 911 emergency call within a reasonable amount of time to extinguish a fire.[4] Similarly, the city paramedics have no duty to respond speedily to a 911 medical emergency call.[5] When an officer fails to arrest a felony suspect, and the suspect flees in a high speed chase that results in a crash that kills an innocent bystander, the police are not liable.[6]

The question remains: when violent crime looms, do the police owe a duty to prevent it?

---

[1] Tex. Civ. Prac. & Rem. Code Ann. § 101.025.

[2] Tex. Civ. Prac. & Rem. Code Ann. § 101.055.

[3] *Fernandez v. City of El Paso*, 876 S.W.2d 370, 375-76 & n. 1 (Tex. App. 1993) (referring to Tex. Civ. Prac. & Rem. Code Ann. § 101.055(2) & (3), § 101.062(b)).

[4] *Id.* at 376-77.

[5] *City of Galveston v. Whitman*, 919 S.W.2d 929, 930-31 (Tex. App. 1996).

[6] *Dent v. City of Dallas*, 729 S.W.2d 114, 116 (Tex. App. 1986).

## *Protective Order Doesn't Protect Child*

Naomi married Quincy Robinson in 1979.[7] Their daughter Melissa was born in 1980. After a history of domestic violence, the couple divorced in June, 1984, and Naomi got a protective order from the court. That protective order prohibited Quincy from committing family violence, directly threatening or harassing any member of the family, and going anywhere near the residence or place of employment of any member of the family.

Quincy ignored that order on October 1, 1984, when he came to Naomi's apartment complex. Naomi called the police, told them about the protective order, told them Quincy was violent, and asked them to stop Quincy. Meanwhile, Quincy captured Melissa and carried her away. When the police came, they said they couldn't do anything about it and left.

Naomi called Quincy at his apartment, and while she spoke to him, her friends (using another phone) called the police again. Naomi was still on the line with Quincy when she heard several gun shots through the phone. When the police arrived at Quincy's apartment, they found that Quincy had murdered young Melissa and then killed himself.

Could Naomi sue the police for failing to enforce the protective order?

Yes, Naomi could sue, and did. Filing a lawsuit is not the same as winning one. The trial court dismissed

---

[7]The facts and law of this case are set forth in *Robinson v. City of San Antonio*, 727 S.W.2d 40 (Tex. App. 1987).

her lawsuit on a motion before trial. The Texas appeals court affirmed that ruling.

The Texas statute shields the city and police for any liability when they fail to provide police protection. The San Antonio Police Department had a policy of enforcing protecting orders which read:

> As violations of Protective Orders are Misdemeanor offenses, officers shall arrest for said violations when an offense is committed in their presence or view, however, if evidence is present to constitute another offense, the person shall be arrested for the highest offense committed.[8]

In this case, however, the court said that the police officers did not personally witness Quincy's violation of the protective order, so they did not have a duty to arrest Quincy. It did not matter that Quincy was known to be violent, and that he had kidnapped his own daughter. On these facts the court said the police had no duty to arrest Quincy without a warrant, and they had no warrant.

In Texas, "no duty" to protect means no duty to enforce a protective order against a violent criminal unless the police see the criminal actually violate that order. When the police simply ignore a dangerous man

---

[8]*Robinson*, 727 S.W.2d at 42, *quoting* General Order 84-8, section 2.04.

who violates the law, how will the police treat *your* 911 emergency call?

# State of Utah

The state and local governmental entities in Utah "are immune from suit for any injury which results from the exercise of a governmental function," with certain exceptions.[1] A "governmental function" is "any act [or] failure to act."[2]

The law makes an exception which allows citizens to sue a governmental entity for the damage caused by a government employee's negligence.[3] Even so, citizens cannot sue the government when its employees negligently perform or fail to perform a "discretionary function," or for failing to prevent or quell mob violence, riots, or civil disturbances.[4]

More to the point, a citizen cannot sue a governmental entity for its negligence in carrying out a "duty owed to the general public."[5] An injured citizen can only sue if the governmental entity owed a duty "to him or her as an individual."[6] In real life, does the government actually owe a duty to protect citizens from violence?

---

[1] Utah Code Ann. § 63-30-3(1).
[2] Utah Code Ann. § 63-30-2(4)(a).
[3] Utah Code Ann. § 63-30-10.
[4] Utah Code Ann. § 63-30-10 (1) & (7).
[5] *Madsen v. Borthick*, 850 P.2d 442, 444 (Utah 1993).
[6] *Id.*

## Released Criminal Psycho Stabs Girl... No Duty

Local government authorities knew about Carolyn Trujillo.[7] In 1981 she was charged in Ogden with assault and disorderly conduct for striking a woman and a child. Trujillo pleaded guilty, but while awaiting sentencing and out on bail, she stabbed an elderly woman in the buttocks in Salt Lake City. Trujillo was charged with aggravated assault, committed to a state mental hospital, and eventually was sentenced to one year probation on a plea bargain that required her to enter a county mental health program.

Trujillo complied with the orders, took her prescribed medication, and was released at the end of her probation. In February 1984, she cut her wrists and was placed in a hospital for psychiatric evaluation and treatment. Trujillo was later transferred to an out-patient therapy program and she attended most of the sessions. The doctors decided she was "stable."

On April 10, 1984, Trujillo was home alone when she heard voices telling her "to stab someone." She took a knife and went looking for a victim. Trujillo found a ten-year old girl whom she knew and stabbed her three times. The slashing severed the young girl's aorta and punctured her stomach.

The little girl survived and, through her mother, sued the governmental entities for negligently failing to properly diagnose, commit, and keep in custody the paranoid schizophrenic Trujillo. No luck. The trial court dismissed the lawsuit, and about 9 years after the

---

[7]The facts and law of this case are set forth in *Higgins v. Salt Lake County*, 855 P.2d 231 (Utah 1993).

brutal attack the Utah Supreme Court affirmed that ruling.

A state or county mental hospital would owe a duty to protect persons who might be harmed by a dangerous mental patient only when the hospital "knew or should have known that unless steps were taken to protect others" from that patient, then the patient was "likely" to cause bodily harm to persons who were "reasonably identifiable" by the hospital. In this case, the state Supreme Court found "that Trujillo never actually distinguished herself from the other potentially dangerous patients by threatening an identifiable victim."

Even if the hospital had owed a duty to discover Trujillo's possible plan to attack that specific young girl, it would not have made any difference to the outcome of the case. State law grants immunity to all the persons performing governmental functions, and a victim cannot sue the government for failing to prevent an assault by another person. The government hospital could not be held liable for failing to prevent the harm to the young girl, even if the government could have discovered that Trujillo might be targeting that girl. Case dismissed.

## State Authorities Know of Escaped Criminal's Plan to Kill... No Duty

Two convicted felons, Von Taylor and Edward Deli, had been serving time in prison but had been transferred to a state-owned "halfway" house.[8] Taylor

---

[8]The facts and law of this case are set forth in *Tiede v. State*, 915 P.2d 500 (Utah 1996).

had a history of violent crime. On December 14, 1990, Taylor and Deli walked away from the halfway house without permission. The two men spent the next week in the mountains near Taylor's father's cabin.

Taylor then phoned a fellow inmate at the halfway house, Scott Manley, at 10:00 a.m. on December 22. Taylor told Manley where he was staying, that he had burglarized other cabins in the area and stolen guns, and that he was waiting for the owners of one cabin to come home. When they came home, Taylor said, he planned to kill them and take their car.

Manley informed officials about Taylor's phone call and his murderous plan. The state officials took no action. At 3:30 p.m. that same afternoon, the owners came home to their cabin. Taylor and Deli then killed the woman and gravely wounded the man who owned the cabin, and then assaulted and kidnapped their two minor daughters. They also killed another woman who came in with the family.

Could the survivors and the estates of the dead victims sue the state for negligently failing to capture Taylor and Deli and failing to protect the victims from those two criminals' vicious attacks? The short answer, according to the Utah Supreme Court, was "no."

If a governmental entity acts negligently, and the negligence results in someone committing assault, battery, or false imprisonment against another person, then under a Utah statute the government cannot be sued.[9] In this case, the negligence of the state

[9]*Tiede*, 915 P.2d at 502-503, *citing* Utah Code Ann. § 63-30-10(2).

authorities resulted in those sorts of wrongs done to the victims and so the state could not be sued.

In addition, the state Supreme Court held that the state could not be held liable for the two deaths. No law allowed a citizen to sue a governmental entity for wrongful death, so no such lawsuit was permitted. Case closed.

The Utah Supreme Court summed it up: "We sympathize with the [victims and the survivors] for the tragedy they have suffered. Nevertheless, we are bound by the legislature's policy decision and are constrained by the immunity act to deny recovery against the State."[10] In other words, when it comes to depending upon the state to protect you, the courts will extend to their sympathy... even when the cops ignore your calls.

---

[10]*Tiede,* 915 P.2d at 504.

# State of Vermont

There is no recent appeals court case in Vermont that explains whether the police owe a duty to protect individual citizens from criminal attack. The Supreme Court of Vermont has held that the following rules apply:

(1) A governmental entity can be liable for having assumed a duty of care toward specific persons, beyond the duty to the general public, if:
   (a) a statute requires the governmental entity to perform certain acts to protect a certain class of persons;
   (b) the governmental entity knows that specific persons within that class are in danger;
   (c) those specific persons have relied on the governmental entity's actions or promises; and
   (d) the governmental entity's failure to carry out that duty would increase the risk of harm to those persons (beyond what their risk was before the governmental entity acted or failed to act).[1]

(2) Lower-level government employees cannot be sued for negligently performing "discretionary acts in good faith during the course of their employment and within the scope of their authority."[2]

---

[1] *Johnson v. State of Vermont*, 682 A.2d 961, 962-63 (Vt. 1996).
[2] *Hudson v. Town of East Montpelier*, 638 A.2d 561, 563 (Vt.

(3) Whether an act is "discretionary" depends upon whether it involves a policy decision based upon the allocation of resources or "a balancing of potential benefits and risks to the public."[3]

Under these three legal principles, it appears that the private citizen would not be able to sue a police officer, police department or city, for failing to protect that citizen from criminal attack. Providing police protection might be considered a "discretionary act," and so might the officer's performance of his or her job. Unless the Vermont legislature passes a law that requires police officers or police departments to protect specific individuals, then no duty to protect will likely exist.[4]

When you dial 911 in Vermont, you can hope the police come. If they don't come and the criminal attacker injures you, then you can expect a lengthy court battle if you want to sue the police. If the attacker kills you, then your heirs will have to decide whether a lawsuit is worthwhile. Maybe it would be better to take advantage of Vermont's laws that allow innocent peaceful citizens to carry concealed firearms

---

1993).

[3]*Id.* at 565-66. *See also Hillerby v. Town of Colchester,* 706 A.2d 446 (Vt. 1997), *corrected* (March 2, 1998) (reaffirming municipal immunity for governmental functions).

[4]*Cf. Sabia v. State of Vermont,* 669 A.2d 1187, 1192 (Vt. 1995) (Department of Social and Rehabilitation Services had a statutory duty to investigate reports of child abuse and render appropriate services, and thus could be sued for failure to protect children at risk of abuse.)

for their protection (without needing government permission)—before you ever need to dial 911.

# Commonwealth of Virginia

Does the government owe a duty to protect citizens in Virginia? Unless there is a provision in the constitution or in a statute that imposes liability on local governments, the general rule is that "a county is not liable for personal injuries caused by the negligence of its officers, agents or employees."[1]

What happens when the county sheriff improperly releases a suspected murderer from jail, and that suspect kills your loved one? Ask the widow Mrs. Lois Marshall.

## *Oops... You're Dead!*

When Mr. Mundy was initially arrested, he was wearing a bullet proof vest and carrying a clip of 50 rounds of ammunition.[2] Mundy told the arresting officer that he could kill that officer because, Mundy said, he had killed another officer already. Mundy was convicted for "possession of a concealed semi-automatic pistol." At the sentencing on February 24, 1987, the judge had reviewed the record and personally expressed concern that Mundy might kill himself or somebody else. Even so, the judge sentenced Mundy to only six months in jail.

Just nine days later, the jailers mistakenly released Mundy. The police arrested Mundy on a related charge

---

[1]*Mann v. County Bd. of Arlington County*, 98 S.E.2d 515 (Va. 1957).

[2]The facts and law of this case are set forth in *Marshall v. Winston*, 389 S.E.2d 902 (Va. 1990).

on March 13, and he was put back into the same jail. Five hours later, Mundy was released again.

The county sheriff and jailer were supposed to protect the public from violent criminals. Twice, however, the sheriff and jailer had improperly released the violent criminal. Mundy was on the loose on April 8, 1987. Jack Marshall was working that night as a hotel's auditor, and he had access to the hotel's money. On that night, Mundy robbed Jack Marshall and killed him.

Mrs. Lois Marshall sued the sheriff and jailer for negligently releasing a prisoner before the expiration of his sentence. A jury never heard her case. The court dismissed Mrs. Marshall's lawsuit on two legal grounds. On appeal the Virginia Supreme Court agreed.

First, a jailer who takes custody of a person and who knows or should know that the person might cause bodily harm to others, does have a duty to use reasonable care to control that person to prevent him from doing any harm. But Mrs. Marshall did not show enough evidence that the sheriff and jailer knew or should have known that Mundy was a person who might harm somebody. Therefore, the Court said, the sheriff and jailer could not be sued for failing to hold Mundy.

Second, the Court held that the sheriff and jailer had a duty to hold Mundy and other prisoners in jail, but that they owed that duty only to the public at large. Only if they owed that duty to a specific identifiable person or class of persons, then they could be sued for failing to do that duty.

Mrs. Marshall was unable to prove that the sheriff and jailer owed a special duty to any particular person or class. There was no "special relationship" between the sheriff or jailer and Mrs. Marshall. Therefore, Mrs. Marshall could not sue these public officials for letting a criminal go free and kill her husband.

## *Parole is for Predators*

Morris Mason was convicted in January 1976 of arson and grand larceny.[3] Mason was sentenced to 20 years, but 10 years were suspended, so he was paroled in April 1978. Mason was released in Northampton County. Two state parole officers were assigned to supervise his parole. The two parole officers knew about Mason's mental instability, his reputation for arson, his sexual aberrations, and his violent antisocial tendencies.

Mason lived up to his reputation. In the first two weeks of May 1978, Mason defrauded an innkeeper, got drunk and made improper sexual advances to women. Mason was convicted of the fraud, which was both a misdemeanor and a parole violation. Mason was sentenced to jail and fined $25. The jail time was suspended.

The parole officers warned Mason not to do anything else to violate his parole, or else he risked returning to prison. Under the law at that time, however, the parole officers were supposed to arrest and jail Mason for the parole violations until a parole hearing could take place. The parole officers themselves did not obey that law.

---

[3]The facts and law of this case are set forth in *Fox v. Custis*, 372 S.E.2d 373 (Va. 1988).

Mason committed murder on May 13. The next day was also busy for Mason. He burned down the house of one woman. He abducted, beat and raped another woman and set her on fire. He shot and stabbed a third woman.

The three women victims sued the state parole officers for failing to arrest Mason for his initial parole violation (as required by law) and for their negligence in failing to adequately supervise Mason's parole. These two failures had led to the women's injuries and damages.

*The women's cases never went to a jury.* The Supreme Court of Virginia held that the parole officers owed no duty to protect these women. There was no "special relation" between the officers and the women that required the officers to control the conduct of a parolee such as Mason. No special relationship existed to require the officers to protect the women from Mason. Cases dismissed.

Although the possibility of criminals being paroled in Virginia has been reduced in recent years, the threat of criminal violence remains. Virginia's general no-duty rule suggests that the police might owe no duty to respond to your 911 call. When in danger of criminal attack, would armed self-defense be more reliable than merely calling the police?

# Virgin Islands

The law of the Virgin Islands draws directly from the American Law Institute's Restatements of the Law and from the "general law" of the United States.[1] Accordingly, the "public duty" doctrine applies in the Virgin Islands: the police owe their duties to the general public, but not to specific individuals, unless there is a "special relationship" between the individuals and the police.[2]

---

[1]V.I. Code Ann. tit. 1, § 4. The ALI Restatements themselves compile the general principles of American common law drawn from judicial decisions in many state jurisdictions.

[2]*Turbe v. Government of the Virgin Islands*, 938 F.2d 427, 429 (3d Cir. 1991) (government cannot be held liable unless there is a special relationship between the government and the citizen, such as when the government action itself increased the risk or caused the damages to the citizen).

# State of Washington

Washington falls in the category of "die first, sue later" jurisdictions. In that state, the police are not immune from being sued.[1] In fact, a Washington statute requires that the sheriff and deputies "shall keep and preserve the peace" and "arrest... all persons who break the peace, or attempt to break it."[2] Under that statute, however, government owes the duty to provide police protection to the public at large, not to individuals.[3]

Washington courts have regularly interpreted the law to allow injured citizens and the heirs of dead citizens to sue police departments for the negligence of their officers.[4] Under Washington law, a private individual can sue the government for failure to provide police protection if:

(1) there is some legal relationship or connection between the police department and the victim which "sets the victim apart from the general public," and

(2) there are "explicit assurances of protection" that cause the victim to rely on those assurances.[5]

---

[1] *Chambers-Castanes v. King County*, 669 P.2d 451, 457 (Wash. 1983) (interpreting Wash Rev. Code § 4.96.010).

[2] Wash. Rev. Code § 36.28.010, as quoted in *Chambers-Castanes*, 669 P.2d at 457.

[3] *Chambers-Castanes*, 669 P.2d at 457; *Beal v. City of Seattle*, 954 P.2d 234 (Wash. App. 1998) (*en banc*) (same rule).

[4] *See Bailey v. Town of Forks*, 737 P.2d 1257 (Wash. 1987).

[5] *Chambers-Castanes*, 669 P.2d at 458.

The following cases show how the rules work in practice.

## *Lies, Excuses, Delays*

As they were driving through town on April 22, 1980, Jim and Steve Ann Chambers-Castanes were stopped momentarily in traffic at 5:50 p.m. [6] Out from the pickup truck in front of them came two men who approached the stopped car. Jim got out to see what the men wanted. Without any reason or warning, both men hit Jim, knocked him down and beat him. One of the men also attacked and struck Steve Ann.

Many witnesses saw the attack and kept track of the two men afterward. Several observers and Steve Ann called the police; the police received 11 calls for assistance from the time of the attacks until the police arrived at 7:12 p.m. After the earliest calls, a police car was dispatched, but it was recalled back when a witness phoned the police to say the people involved in the fight had left the area.

More calls came into the police department. Steve Ann called about 30 minutes after the attack to complain that, after 4 calls by others, no police had arrived. Steve Ann was injured and emotionally upset, so the police operator said "You'd better calm down or I won't send anybody." Later in the call, the operator said a police officer would be sent over—but no officer was actually dispatched.

A few minutes later, as helpful witnesses started to surround and corner the attackers on foot, Steve Ann

---

[6]The facts and law of this case are set forth in *Chambers-Castanes v. King County*, 669 P.2d 451 (Wash. 1983).

called the police again. The dispatcher told her again that a police officer was on the way, but still none had been dispatched. After several calls by others, a police officer was dispatched at 6:56 p.m. The police finally arrived at 7:12 p.m. By then, the attackers had escaped.

Jim and Steve Ann sued the police department and city government agencies. The trial court dismissed their suit, but three years after the attack, the Supreme Court of Washington decided that the suit would be allowed to proceed to a trial. The transcript of the telephone calls showed that the police dispatcher had assured Steve Ann that help was on the way, and Jim and Steve Ann had relied on the police to come. These facts were enough to support a lawsuit against the police.

Having enough facts to support a lawsuit does not mean that Jim and Steve Ann had won anything but their day in court. They had no guarantee of winning. The attackers, who could have been sued for personal injury damages, were never found, largely because the police arrived so late.

## Is This An Emergency Or Are You Drunk?

Shirley and Marie Noakes, developmentally disabled mother and daughter, were living in Seattle together, when on March 18, 1990, just after midnight, William Jimerson began breaking into their home.[7] Over a 9 to

---

[7]The case and law of this case are set forth in *Noakes v. City of Seattle*, 895 P.2d 842 (Wash. App. 1995).

11 minute period, they called 911 three times to report the invasion as it was unfolding.

On the first call, the operator asked Shirley whether she was drunk, and then told Shirley that she would "send someone out." The second time the women called, they were told the police department was handling 15 calls waiting for help, but that they would send someone as soon as they could. Marie, in the third call, told the operator that she didn't care whom they sent, "somebody, anybody, even a medic." Marie explained that the "prowler" was breaking the bedroom window and was about to enter the house. The operator on this call asked Marie if she had been drinking.

Jimerson got inside their room, was acting crazy, assaulted and raped the two defenseless women. Thirty minutes after their last 911 call, a dispatcher called the women's residence to see if they still needed help. It was too late by then, as Jimerson was still there and had already threatened and raped the women. In fear for her safety, Shirley told the dispatcher that the prowler was gone and to cancel the call.

Over an hour later, Marie escaped Jimerson and ran to a neighbor's house to dial 911 again. The police did not arrive. The neighbor called 911 one more time, telling the dispatcher that there was a man in the victims' house, Marie was injured and Shirley was still inside. Finally, the police came and arrested the attacker.

Jimerson was convicted of the rape and assault of the two women. Shirley and Marie sued the city police department for negligently failing to respond to their emergency call. The trial court initially dismissed their lawsuit, but the state appeals court reversed that decision so that the case could go to trial.

The Washington appeals court decided that the 911 operator's saying they would send someone out to help might be enough to prove that the police gave an "express assurance" of help. The fact that the two women stayed in their home during the attack, instead of taking some other self-defense action, showed that they at least minimally relied on the "assurance" that police were on the way. A jury would ultimately decide in a trial whether the city police were negligent.

The right to sue a police department, after you are robbed, hurt or dead, and at your own expense, is perhaps a form of legal protection. Is it the best defense to criminal attack?

# State of West Virginia

West Virginia embraces the "public duty" doctrine. Under that doctrine, a local government generally cannot be held liable for failing to carry out its duty to protect individual citizens, because the government owes that duty to only the public at large.[1] A West Virginia statute also immunizes government from liability for "the failure to provide, or the method of providing police, law enforcement or fire protection."[2]

An exception exists where there is a "special relationship" between the victim and the police. After the crime victim has suffered injury, the victim (or the heirs of the victim) can sue the police department if the evidence proves these four facts existed before the victim was injured:

(1) The local police, by its promises or actions, undertook a duty to act on behalf of the victim;

(2) the local police knew that their failure to act could lead to harm to the victim;

(3) there was some form of direct contact between the police and the injured victim; and

(4) the victim had justifiably relied on the police's undertaking the duty to help or protect the victim.[3]

---

[1]*Randall v. City of Fairmont Police Dept.*, 412 S.E.2d 737, 747-48 (W. Va. 1991).

[2]W.Va. Code § 29-12A-5(a)(5) (1986), *quoted in Randall*, 412 S.E.2d at 741 n.1.

[3]*Wolfe v. City of Wheeling*, 387 S.E.2d 307, 311 (W.Va. 1989).

To date there are no published judicial decisions about whether police in West Virginia can be liable for failing to properly respond to a 911 distress call. Two recent cases suggest how the courts might rule. Would you trust these legal opinions to protect you and your loved ones?

## *Death In The Police Parking Lot*

Zachary Lewis had been harassing and threatening Sandra Johnson, and he had so injured her that she required hospitalization.[4] Sandra called the police at least four times in mid-1988 to report these crimes. She told the police that she feared for her life.

Criminal charges were filed against Lewis. When he failed to appear in court the judge issued a warrant for his arrest. Despite the outstanding arrest warrant and Sandra's numerous calls to the police about Lewis' threats against her, the police did nothing to stop or arrest Lewis.

Sandra was driving her car through town when she noticed Lewis following her. She was afraid, so she drove to the police station and parked her car directly beside the police department building. Lewis followed her into the parking lot. Sandra blew her car horn many times, trying to get the police officers' attention.

No police officers or anyone else responded to the frantically honking horn. Lewis got out of his car, walked to Sandra's car, and shot and killed Sandra. He also shot and injured a passenger. These bloody crimes emotionally traumatized a third person in the car.

---

[4]The facts and law of this case are set forth in *Randall v. City of Fairmont Police Dept.,* 412 S.E.2d 737 (W. Va. 1991).

Sandra's child was delivered shortly later from her body by Caesarean section, but the child also died two months later.

Sandra died on August 15, 1988. The West Virginia Supreme Court of Appeals decided on December 12, 1991, that her heirs could lawfully sue the police department for negligence on these facts. The key facts that apparently convinced the Court were that (1) Sandra had contacted the police several times about threats, (2) the police did not try to arrest Lewis even on the outstanding warrant, and (3) the killing took place in the police parking lot.

Sandra's heirs "won" in the high court, but that did not mean they had "won" their case against the police. The victory meant only that the heirs could pursue the lawsuit further, at their own expense, to a jury trial. Even if the heirs won a jury verdict, post-trial motions and future appeals would quite possibly delay or deny them an ultimate victory. Sandra and her baby, meanwhile, remain dead without appeal.

## No "Contact," No "Reliance," No Case

Deborah Semple had a long-term relationship with Michael Suarez and bore two children by him: Amanda and Angela.[5] Michael exhibited a violent nature, and Deborah had filed a battery charge against him in 1989, but withdrew it. Deborah's mother had called the police six times between January and June, 1994, to report Michael's abusing Deborah. On June 21, 1994,

---

[5]The facts and law of this case are set forth in *Semple v. City of Moundsville*, 963 F. Supp. 1416 (N.D.W.Va. 1997).

Deborah herself called the police about Michael's abusing her and the danger he presented to her and the two girls.

The police responded, helped Deborah remove the children from the home, and advised her of her rights as a domestic abuse victim. The same day, Deborah obtained a temporary protective order against Michael which directed him not to contact, call, harass, or abuse her. The police said they would promptly serve the order; they failed to do so.

Deborah called the police two days later to report Michael had taken her car. Michael called the police himself and was told about the court order, but even though they knew where he was, the police did not formally serve him with it. The police told Deborah's mother that they would arrest Michael if he violated the terms of the order, however.

The next day, Deborah informed the police that Michael had been at her residence in violation of the order. The police said they would dispatch an extra patrol for her. That same day the local court issued a final order against Michael and advised the police that they could arrest and jail Michael for any violation.

Two days later, Deborah's mother called the police again about Michael at the residence. The police found that Michael had broken a window, entered the residence, threatened Deborah and hit her in the head with a gun, attempted to choke her and threatened to kill her. They served him with the court's order, jailed him, and charged him with felony and misdemeanor violent crimes. Michael's bail was set at $75,000, with the condition that he obey the court order.

Deborah quickly moved herself and her children to her mother's home. Michael posted bond and was released on July 1. The police notified Deborah that Michael had been released. Five days later, Deborah reported to police that Michael had been telephonically harassing her and her family. She filed a criminal complaint against Michael and a warrant was issued for his arrest.

That same day Michael was arrested at the rear of Deborah's mother's home where he had been harassing her. Despite the record of violations of the protective order and pending criminal charges, Michael was released on a $500 bond.

On August 6, Deborah returned to her previous residence with her two daughters, her brother Scott, and her friend James. Scott was carrying a loaded handgun. At 1:30 p.m. she called police to inform them that Michael had vandalized the residence, but she did not request assistance. At 1:43 p.m., however, Deborah frantically called police and told them that Michael was in the house. Three minutes later, the police arrived to find Michael had murdered Deborah, Scott and James, and then killed himself.

The heirs of the victims sued the police department and the city on several grounds, one of which was the negligence of the police in failing to protect the victims from Michael. The federal district court dismissed the entire case and all claims.[6]

---

[6]The heirs also sued on grounds that the victims' federal civil and constitutional rights had been violated. All of these claims were dismissed as well. *Semple,* 963 F. Supp. at 1424-34.

The heirs of Scott and James could not sue the police because Scott and James had never personally contacted the police about Michael. The police never made any promises to protect them. As the victims had no "special relationship" with the police, the police owed them no duty to protect them as individuals.

## Protect Yourself, And You're On Your Own

Deborah, Scott and James also never "justifiably relied" on any promise of police protection. Under West Virginia law, a "special relationship can exist only where the police have taken some action to create in an individual a false sense of security, have caused an individual to relax his own vigilance or have caused an individual to forego other available avenues of protection."[7] James had never contacted the police, so the police never lulled him into a false sense of security.

Scott was carrying a loaded handgun when he ventured back into Deborah's previous residence. He was not "relying" upon police promises of protection.

Deborah had previously moved out of the residence, rather than staying in the residence and relying upon police protection there. When she returned to the residence, she was accompanied by two adult men, one of whom was armed. On the day she was killed by Michael, Deborah was not relying on past promises of the police to protect her. As she was not relying on the police, there was no "special relationship" which would allow her heirs to obtain damages from the police.

___

[7]*Semple*, 963 F. Supp. at 1435, *citing Wolfe*, 387 S.E.2d at 311.

The criminal justice system failed Deborah, and the police owed no duty to protect her. Her frantic 911 call to the police was to be her last.

# State of Wisconsin

A Wisconsin statute declares that the cities and their police officers ordinarily cannot be sued for negligently failing to protect individual citizens.[1] The general rule "in Wisconsin is that a public officer or employee is immune from personal liability for injuries resulting from acts performed within the scope of the individual's public office."[2]

There are three exceptions to this rule. The public officer has no immunity if (1) he engages in malicious, willful or intentional misconduct; (2) he negligently performs a "ministerial duty;" or (3) he knows of a danger that is of "such a quality" that the officer's "duty to act becomes absolute, certain and imperative."

For young Shannon Barillari, the general rule and its exceptions were no help.[3]

## Bet Your Life On A Promise?

Shannon Barillari had been dating Charles Estergard for about two years, but tried to break off with him in July 1987. Estergard responded by threatening to commit suicide, and on July 29, he sexually assaulted Shannon at knife point. To avoid further harm, Shannon told Estergard she would move in with him the following day, and that he should pick her up at her mother's house.

---

[1]Wis. Stat. § 893.80(4).

[2]*Barillari v. City of Milwaukee*, 533 N.W.2d 759, 763 (Wis. 1995).

[3]*Id.*

The next morning, July 30, Shannon told her mother and sister about the assault, then went to the hospital where doctors examined her, and the police took photographs of her injuries as evidence for charges against Estergard. Shannon's mother told the police that she feared Estergard would again attack Shannon. The police detective promised that Estergard would not get near Shannon because the police would immediately obtain a warrant for his arrest and would capture Estergard when he came to Shannon's home that day.

The police detective started the legal processes necessary to get authority to arrest Estergard. Estergard, however, did not show up and was not arrested on July 30. The following day, after meeting with Shannon and her mother, the assistant district attorney decided to give Estergard a few days to turn himself in.

Estergard was not arrested and did not turn himself in. On August 4, 1987, Estergard went to Shannon's house. He first shot Shannon and then himself.

Shannon's family sued the city (as employer of the police department and officers) for negligence. The family argued that the police detectives had *promised* to arrest Estergard or to tell the family that he had not been arrested. Also, the family had previously planned to leave the Milwaukee area so they could avoid Estergard's threatened violence, but because they *relied* on the police assurances the family had stayed in town.

Under Wisconsin law, however, Shannon had no enforceable right to police protection. The detective's promise to arrest Estergard was not binding. The family's reliance on the assurance of protection was worthless. Thus, her family was not allowed to sue for damages arising from the police failure to protect Shannon.

The Supreme Court of Wisconsin explained why the police could not be liable for protecting individual crime victims:

> We look to our police departments to enforce our laws and to maintain order in what is becoming an increasingly dangerous society. Routinely, police face critical situations, many of which have the potential for violence. On a typical day, any given law enforcement officer may be arresting and questioning suspects, interviewing and counseling victims, talking to witnesses, rescuing children, and investigating criminal activity. In the course of their work, police must often try to console and reassure people who are distraught and fearful. Faced with escalating violence, they must continuously use their discretion to set priorities and decide how best to handle specific incidents. Police officers must be free to perform their responsibilities, using their experience, training, and good judgment, without also fearing that they or their employer could be held liable for damages from their allegedly negligent discretionary decisions.[4]

The Wisconsin Court admitted that the state and local governments cannot adequately protect their citizens, even when the police know who the violent criminals are and whom they have threatened to hurt.

---

[4]*Barillari*, 533 N.W.2d at 764-65.

The police cannot do the whole job, the Court said, and should not be liable for damages when they negligently fail.

The Court offers no help to citizens in danger, and no compensation for those victims killed or injured by criminals. Meanwhile, "gun control" laws discourage people from owning and using firearms to protect themselves. Had Shannon Barillari been armed when Estergard came to her door, would she have had a better chance of being alive today?

## *County Officials Fail To Protect Abused Boy... No Duty*

A heartbreaking case from Wisconsin led to the landmark United States Supreme Court decision *DeShaney v. Winnebago County Department of Social Services.*[5] A young boy, Joshua DeShaney, was the victim of severe child abuse at the hands of his father over a period of about three years. After the father and mother were divorced, the father was awarded custody of Joshua who was only a year old. The father soon remarried but divorced again.

County authorities learned in January 1982 from the father's second wife that the father was abusing Joshua. Winnebago County (Wisconsin) Department of Social Services (DSS) interviewed the father about these accusations, but dropped the investigation when he denied them. A year later Joshua was admitted to a hospital with multiple bruises and scrapes. The examining doctor suspected child abuse, notified DSS,

---

[5]*DeShaney v. Winnebago County Dep't of Soc. Servs.*, 489 U.S. 189, 109 S. Ct. 998 (1989).

and immediately Joshua was taken out of his father's custody for a few days.

A "child protection team," essentially a committee of several professionals, decided that there was not enough evidence of child abuse to retain custody of Joshua. They returned Joshua to his father, on condition that Joshua be enrolled in preschool, the father undergo counseling, and the new live-in girlfriend move out. A month later Joshua was back in the hospital with suspicious injuries. The DSS caseworker decided there was no basis for action against the father.

For the following six months, the DSS caseworker visited Joshua's home about 20 times and observed suspicious injuries. Joshua had not been enrolled in preschool, and the girlfriend was still in the house. The caseworker logged these facts along with her suspicions of child abuse, but took no action to protect Joshua. In November, 1983, a hospital emergency room notified DSS about suspected abuse of Joshua. On the caseworker's next two visits to the home, she was not permitted to see the boy because he was "too ill." Neighbors had reported suspicious beatings of Joshua to DSS. With all of this information, DSS still took no action to take custody of Joshua and protect him from further harm.

In March, 1984, the father beat four-year-old Joshua so badly that he bled into the brain, fell into a coma, and suffered serious, permanent and disabling brain damage. Joshua will likely spend the rest of his life in an institution for the profoundly retarded.

On Joshua's behalf his mother sued DSS and the county government for depriving Joshua of his liberty without due process[6] by failing to protect Joshua from the risk of violent injury at the hands of his father, when DSS knew or should have known of that risk.

The legal approach of the lawsuit was a creative attempt to get justice for Joshua. Yet Joshua's case was never heard by a jury. The federal district court judge dismissed the case, and the Seventh Circuit Court of Appeals affirmed that ruling. The Supreme Court also affirmed and declared that:

*Nothing in the language of the Due Process Clause itself requires the State to protect the life, liberty, and property of its citizens against invasion by private actors.* The Clause is phrased as a limitation on the State's power to act, not as a guarantee of certain minimal levels of safety and security. It forbids the State itself to deprive individuals of life, liberty, or property without "due process of law," but its language cannot fairly be extended to impose an affirmative obligation on the State to ensure that those interests do not come to harm through other means.[7]

The purpose of the Due Process Clause was to limit the powers of state governments, not to impose particular duties upon them. Thus the Court explained:

---

[6]The Fourteenth Amendment to the United States Constitution provides that no State may "deprive any person of life, liberty, or property without due process of law."

[7]*DeShaney,* 489 U.S. at 195 (italics added, internal citations omitted).

the Due Process Clauses generally confer no affirmative right to governmental aid, even where such aid may be necessary to secure life, liberty, or property interests of which the government itself may not deprive the individual. []⁸

A state generally cannot be held liable to crime victims under the Due Process Clause because that Clause does not impose a duty on the state to protect its citizens. The Court wrote:

> If the Due Process Clause does not require the State to provide its citizens with particular protective services, it follows that the State cannot be held liable under the Clause for injuries that could have been averted had it chosen to provide them. As a general matter, then, we conclude that a State's failure to protect an individual against private violence simply does not constitute a violation of the Due Process Clause.⁹

## *State Law Rendered Child Defenseless*

Joshua's tragic case is similar to the "dial 911" cases on one point that Justice Brennan highlighted in his dissenting opinion. In his view, "if a State cuts off private sources of aid and then refuses aid itself, it cannot wash its hands of the harm that results from its inaction."¹⁰ The same logic could apply in "dial 911" cases where the citizen is unarmed and relying solely

---

⁸*Id.*, 489 U.S. at 196 (internal citations omitted).
⁹*Id.*, 489 U.S. at 196-197.
¹⁰*Id.*, 489 U.S. at 207 (Brennan, J., dissenting).

upon protection from the government, yet the government denies any duty to protect the citizen.

As Justice Brennan also explained, Wisconsin had "established a child-welfare system specifically designed to help children like Joshua."[11] All of the information about potential child abuse, whether from private, medical or police sources, was channeled to DSS. "In this way, Wisconsin law invites—indeed, directs—citizens and other governmental entities to depend upon" county DSS agencies "to protect children from abuse."[12]

Justice Brennan pointed out that the DSS controlled whether Joshua were taken into protective custody or returned to (and kept in) the abusive home.[13] Joshua could not control his fate; he could not protect himself. The Wisconsin governmental entities did not just abandon him, *they actively placed him where they knew he defenselessly faced repeated criminal attack.*

No one was there for Joshua. Not the social workers, not the doctors, not the police, and not the Supreme Court. And unlike an adult victim who could feasibly obtain and use a weapon, Joshua had no means to protect himself whatsoever. Would it ever make sense for *adults* to place themselves in Joshua's predicament: defenseless and relying solely upon the grace of governmental entities and law for protection?

---

[11]*Id.*, 489 U.S. at 208.

[12]*Id.*

[13]*Id.*, 489 U.S. at 209.

# State of Wyoming

Wyoming is one state where government employees are generally immune from lawsuits.[1] Yet Wyoming also has a law that expressly allows citizens to sue governmental entities for the negligence of peace officers:

> A governmental entity is liable for damages resulting from tortious conduct of peace officers while acting within the scope of their duties.[2]

Even though the statute appears to clearly state a rule that makes the city liable for negligence of police officers, at least up to a limit of $250,000 per person and $500,000 per accident,[3] the courts still carve exceptions for police who fail to protect citizens.

Read the following two cases, and then try to predict whether the Wyoming Supreme Court would impose a duty upon police to respond adequately to your emergency call.

## *Not Drunk Enough... No Duty*

The Torrington Police officer saw a sporty red car parked at a bar after midnight on June 15, 1988.[4] At about 2:15 a.m. the officer saw the red car driving through town with a burned-out headlight. Seeing an

---

[1]Wyo. Stat. Ann. § 1-39-104.

[2]Wyo. Stat. Ann. § 1-39-112.

[3]Wyo. Stat. Ann. § 1-39-118.

[4]The facts and law of this case are set forth in *Keehn v. Town of Torrington*, 834 P.2d 112 (Wyo. 1992).

opportunity to check the driver for driving under the influence of alcohol, the officer followed the red car for over half a mile but saw no suspicious driving behavior. The officer decided to stop the red car because of the burned-out headlight.

The driver of the red car did not show signs of intoxication, either in his speech or his movements. There was a general smell of alcohol coming from the car which contained three passengers. As the officer was writing up the ticket for the headlight, a dispatch call came in about some broken glass reported and a stolen car. Deciding to investigate those incidents instead, the officer never finished the ticket but simply warned the driver to get the light fixed. The officer left the driver to continue on his way at about 2:24 a.m.

About two hours later, the red car crossed over the center and crashed head-on with an oncoming car. Three people were killed: two passengers in the red car and the driver of the oncoming car. A blood test showed that the red car's driver had a blood alcohol content of 0.13 percent. Under Wyoming law, it was illegal to drive with a blood alcohol content of 0.10 percent or more.[5]

The survivors of the dead victims sued the city, saying that the officer had negligently failed to enforce the drunk driving law. Peace officers in Wyoming have a legal duty to arrest and remove drunk drivers from the road. That law exists to protect the public at large (and the passengers in the car) from the risks of drunk driving.

[5]Wyo. Stat. Ann. § 31-5-233.

It turns out, however, that it was legal to drink and drive in Wyoming if you did so "safely." As the Wyoming Supreme Court also pointed out, the United States and Wyoming Constitutions protect people from being searched or arrested without probable cause, and an officer cannot detain a person without a reasonable suspicion that the person is involved in criminal activity. The officer in this case had no real evidence that the driver had been drinking, so he let the driver go.

The officer had a duty to take drunk drivers off the road, and had failed to do so in this case. The trial court and state Supreme Court both held that "reasonable minds" would all agree that the officer had not acted negligently.

Perhaps the courts were right: even careful police officers sometimes make mistakes and sometimes don't detect criminal behavior. Police officers are not perfect. Moreover, as the state Supreme Court pointed out, "governments simply do not have the resources to protect all citizens at all times from the consequences of all illegal or tortious activity."[6]

If the police cannot be expected to protect you and your family, then who is ultimately responsible for providing that protection?

## *Police Place Drunk and Disturbed Convicted Felon In Cab*

If you cannot trust the police, whom can you trust? Police officers in the City of Sheridan came upon

---

[6]*Keehn*, 834 P.2d at 116.

Danny Welch on April 8, 1992.[7] The police knew Danny to be a convicted felon just out of prison, and they found him drunk and "emotionally upset and disturbed." The police did not arrest Danny, even though he was under the legal age for drinking. Danny had no where to go, he said, so the police took him to the police station. Danny made some calls but did not reach any friends to help him.

The police dispatcher called a taxicab for Danny. When the female driver picked up Danny at the station in her cab, the police still did not know where Danny intended to go, who the person at the destination address was, or what the telephone number was. Apparently the police expected Danny to tell the driver later. The police never told the driver about Danny's criminal record, his being drunk, his showing signs of emotional disturbance, or that they did not know anything about Danny's intended destination.

Danny kidnapped and raped the cab driver. She sued the police officers and their employer, the city, for negligently failing to warn her about the dangers presented by Danny, and for failing to take steps to minimize those dangers.

Deciding a pre-trial motion, the trial court dismissed the driver's lawsuit on the grounds that the officers were immune from suit. A peace officer is held to be immune from suit if the officer has performed "discretionary" duties reasonably and in good faith.[8]

---

[7] The facts and law of this case are set forth in *Darrar v. Bourke*, 910 P.2d 572 (Wyo. 1996).

[8] *Id.* at 575-76.

The trial court held that the officers had carried out their discretionary duties reasonably and in good faith.

On appeal, the Wyoming Supreme Court disagreed only to a certain extent. That Court held that there was not enough evidence in the case to decide whether the officers had acted reasonably or that their duties were "discretionary." The Court therefore referred the case back to the trial court to obtain more evidence. The injured victim had "won" only the opportunity to continue the lawsuit until more evidence was brought out. The officers and the city might still persuade the court to dismiss the driver's case, or failing that, they might convince a jury that the officers had acted reasonably.

Would the outcome of the whole situation have been different if the taxicab driver had been carrying a concealed firearm? Would she have been safer trusting her firearms skills than trusting the police who placed a drunken criminal in her cab?

# Canada

In what cases do the police in Canada owe a duty to protect private citizens from criminal attack? The answer is quite uncertain. Canadian courts recognize the general rule that the police do not "owe a general duty of care to individual members of the public to identify and apprehend an unknown criminal."[1] On the other hand, when the police have specific facts about a particular criminal's predatory habits and have good reason to suspect in what locality or neighborhood the criminal is likely to strike next, then the police will owe a duty to warn the potential victims in that area.[2]

Basically, the general rule in Canada is that the police are not liable to protect any particular member of the public unless the risk of criminal attack is "foreseeable" and there is a "special relationship" created by the victim's reasonably relying upon the police for protection.[3]

---

[1]*Doe v. Toronto (Metropolitan) Commissioners of Police,* [1989] O.J. No. 471, quoting the British House of Lords decision in *Hill v. Chief Constable of West Yorkshire,* [1988] 2 E.R. 238 (H.L.), *affirming* [1987] 1 All E.R. 1173 (C.A.).

[2]*Doe v. Toronto (Metropolitan) Commissioners of Police,* 58 D.L.R. (4th) 396, [1989] O.J. No. 471, *affirmed by* 74 O.R. (2d) 225, 72 D.L.R. (4th) 580 (1990).

[3]*See Kamloops (City) v. Nielsen,* [1984] 2 S.C.R. 2, 66 B.C.L.R. 273, 29 C.C.L.T. 97, 8 C.L.R. 1, 10 D.L.R. (4th) 641, 26 M.P.L.R. 81, 54 N.R. 1, [1984] 5 W.W.R. 1.

## Police Failed To Protect Potential
## Rape Victim... Victim Wins Damages

In one celebrated case, a rape victim sued the police for failing to protect her from a serial rapist.[4] Ten years after she filed her lawsuit and after a trial in which she received damages against the police, a Canadian appellate court affirmed that the police owed her a duty on several grounds. Following is the case summary written by the Canadian court, edited to enhance readability.

In the early morning hours of August 24, 1986, Ms. Doe, who lived in a second-floor apartment in the Church and Wellesley area of Toronto, was raped at knifepoint by PDC, who had broken into her apartment from a balcony. At the time, Ms. Doe was the fifth victim of similar crimes by PDC, who would become known as the "balcony rapist".

It wasn't just that Ms. Doe was attacked and raped by a serial rapist; the police virtually allowed the crime to take place:

The evidence at trial established that, before the rape of Ms. Doe, PDC had committed similar crimes on December 31, 1985, January 10, 1986, June 25, 1986, and July 25, 1986. All the crimes took place in apartment residences in the Church and Wellesley area of the City of Toronto. By August of 1986,

---

[4]The facts, and all quoted statements of facts and law, are found in *Doe v. Metropolitan Toronto (Municipality) Commissioners of Police*, 39 O.R. (3d) 487, [1998] O.J. No. 2681.

members of the police force had deduced that the crimes were linked and that the assailant lived in the area of the crimes. They knew that there was most likely a serial rapist attacking women who lived alone in second- and third-floor apartments with climbable balconies and that the rapist would most certainly attack again, likely around the 24th or 25th of the month. However, only two officers, Sgts. C and D, were assigned to the investigation, and they were extremely busy with substantial commitments to other cases.

The police officers decided not to warn any of the potential victims about the risk:

Sergeants C and D decided that their investigation would be low-key in comparison to the approach used by the force in the investigation of another series of rapes, the "Annex Rapist" crimes, in another area of the city, where a task force had been established and where there had been substantial media coverage and publicity of the crimes. With respect to the balcony rapist crimes, Sgts. C and D decided not to issue any warning, and they decided that any increased police presence in the area of the crimes would be made only covertly. Sergeants C and D both testified that they did not want a media blitz alerting the public to the danger because they did not wish the assailant to flee as had the Annex Rapist before his arrest in Vancouver.

The police did not try to warn the likely targets of the serial rapist. Thus,

> Ms. Doe sued the Metropolitan Toronto Police Force for damages on the grounds that (1) the police force had conducted a negligent investigation and failed to warn women of the risk of an attack by PDC; and (2) the police force had violated her rights under Sections 7 and 15 of the Canadian Charter of Rights and Freedoms.

The Canadian court upheld the judgment of damages for Ms. Doe, giving the following reasons:

(1) "The police are statutorily obligated to prevent crime, and, at common law, they owe a duty to protect life and property."

(2) The police utterly failed to carry out their duty to protect Ms. Doe from the serial rapist by failing to warn her so that she could have taken "steps to protect" herself.

(3) According to the evidence given at trial, the police did not give the warning because the officers believed the "women living in the area would become hysterical and scare off the offender and this would jeopardize the investigation." Moreover, the police did not regard the "balcony rapist crimes" to be as serious as the more violent "Annex Rapist crimes." The court found the police's views to be "sexist stereotypical views."

(4) The police failed to protect Ms. Doe because of these "sexist stereotypical views," and therefore they denied Ms. Doe "equal protection" of the law because of her being female.[5]

(5) The police "were aware of the risk" to Ms. Doe "but deliberately failed to inform her of it." The police "exercised their discretion" in a "discriminatory and negligent way." Accordingly, the police violated Ms. Doe's constitutional right to "security of the person" by "subjecting her to the very real risk of attack by a serial rapist."[6]

Ms. Doe received a damage award of over $200,000 (Canadian)... 10 years after the attack and injuries that might have been prevented if only the police had warned her of the risk. In a future case where there is no element of sexist attitudes and discrimination, and where there is no serial criminal with a regular pattern of attack, will the Canadian courts again hold the police liable for negligently failing to protect? Or will they stand on the no-duty rule?

Ms. Doe dialed 911 *after* she was attacked.[7] The police responded to that call to investigate the crime. But what if Ms. Doe had been armed and able to drive the attacker away by herself? And would this serial

---

[5]Canadian Charter of Rights and Freedoms § 15(1) (right to equal benefit and protection of law).

[6]*Id.*, § 7 (right to security of the person).

[7]*See Doe*, 39 O.R. (3d) 487.

rapist have ventured into a neighborhood known for its _well-armed_ single women?

# Your First, Last, and Best Defense

This book has shown dozens of cases where police were either unwilling, unable, or too inept to protect citizens from violent criminals. If the police cannot or will not protect citizens, then who will?

The citizens themselves can and must protect themselves—and they can do it well. All they need are three things.

First, they need the right tools. Second, they need basic familiarity with those tools. Third, they need the legal authority to use those tools for self-defense, *i.e.* they need to be assured that they won't be sued, fined, or jailed for possessing those tools and using them to prevent crime.

## *Defensive Use of Firearms*

Against violent attackers, the best tool for self defense is the simple firearm. Americans use firearms every day to defend their lives and property. Professor Gary Kleck, on faculty at the Florida State University school of criminology and criminal justice, has carefully studied how frequently guns are used to prevent or stop crime.[1] His most recent research shows that law-abiding citizens use guns to defend themselves against criminals as many as 2.5 million times every year.[2] That figure amounts to over 6,850 times per day.[3]

---

[1] Gary Kleck, *Point Blank: Guns and Violence in America* (1991).

[2] Gary Kleck and Marc Gertz, *Armed Resistance to Crime: The Prevalence and Nature of Self-Defense with a Gun*, 86 J. Crim. L. &

The National Institute of Justice estimated that guns were used defensively 1.5 million times each year.[4] The absolute lowest estimate of defensive use of guns, which came from a limited sampling of mostly persons who were victimized while away from their homes, is 108,000 times per year.[5] By these estimates, guns are used anywhere from 2.5 to 60 times more often to protect lives than to take lives wrongfully. Accidents, murders and suicides committed with guns account for fewer than 40,000 lives lost each year.[6]

About 10 percent of the defensive gun uses are women defending themselves against sexual abuse.[7] Self-defense is no toothless tiger: private citizens shoot and kill more criminals (1,527) than do the police (606).[8]

But the overwhelming majority of defensive uses of firearms do not involve any injuries at all. Just

---

Criminology 164 (1995).

[3]An excellent collection of facts about firearms use is available from Gun Owners Foundation, 8001 Forbes Place, Suite 102, Springfield, VA 22151, or on the website at *www.gunowners.org*. Many of the facts cited in this chapter were published in the *GOA Fact Sheet: 1999 Firearms Facts* available at that website.

[4]Philip J. Cook and Jens Ludwig, *Guns in America: National Survey on Private Ownership and Use of Firearms*, Research in Brief (National Institute of Justice: May 1997) (available at *www.ncjrs.org*).

[5]*Id., citing* Bureau of Justice Statistics, National Crime Victimization Survey.

[6]National Safety Council, *Accident Facts* (1997).

[7]Kleck and Gertz, *Armed Resistance to Crime*, at 185.

[8]Kleck, *Point Blank*, at 111-116, 148.

brandishing the weapon, or firing a warning shot, is enough to scare off most attackers.[9]

## *Unseen Guns Drive Criminals Away*

Citizens frequently use weapons to defend themselves, but that is only part of the picture. It is easier to observe and count what actually happens, than it is to measure how often something does *not* happen.[10] How many times do criminals choose *not* to commit a violent crime because they are afraid that the victim might be armed?

That question is difficult to answer because it is hard to count crimes that never occur. Common experience suggests that a rational person would not take the risk of being shot if that person could achieve his goal without that risk. All other things being equal, criminals likely would choose to rob an unarmed person instead of a person carrying a firearm. In one survey, most convicted felons agreed that "a criminal is not going to mess around with a victim he knows is armed with a gun."[11]

What if the criminals aren't sure whether their potential victims are armed? Would the uncertainty itself deter some criminals? Professor John R. Lott, Jr., at the University of Chicago, studied these questions in his landmark research in 1996. Professor Lott

---

[9]Kleck and Gertz, *Armed Resistance to Crime*, at 173, 185.

[10]For an extraordinarily clear discussion of this concept in the field of human action, see Henry Hazlitt, *Economics in One Lesson* 15-24 (2d ed., 1979).

[11]U.S. Department of Justice, National Institute of Justice, *The Armed Criminal in America: A Survey of Incarcerated Felons*, Research Report (July 1985), at 27.

243

examined data from over 3,000 counties over a period of 18 years, looking for a statistical connection between laws that readily permit citizens to carry concealed firearms and the violent crime rate.[12]

The results were startling, but entirely reasonable. States which enacted laws to allow citizens to easily obtain a permit to carry concealed weapons enjoyed these results:[13]

- Murders decreased by 8.5%
- Rapes decreased by 5%
- Aggravated assaults decreased by 7%
- Robbery decreased by 3%

Statistics and common sense suggest that when the peace-loving and virtuous citizens arm themselves, they accomplish two things: (1) they prepare for, and are able to carry out, self-defense against criminal aggression, and (2) by being armed and prepared, they deter many criminals from committing violent crimes.

Consider the opposite view. Is it sensible to say that *unarmed* individuals can defend themselves better against criminals? Is it reasonable to suppose that

---

[12]John R. Lott, Jr., *More Guns, Less Crime: Understanding Crime and Gun Control Laws* (University of Chicago Press, 1998).

[13]Aggregated estimates taken from John R. Lott, Jr., *More Guns, Less Violent Crime*, Wall Street Journal, August 28, 1996.

criminals will *avoid unarmed people*, but will try to kill, rape, or rob only people with firearms?

# Forty-Five Stories With Happy Endings

Rather than relying solely on the police to protect them, thousands of Americans successfully defend themselves and others from violence. Sometimes defense requires just pointing a firearm at the attacker, other times the defender must shoot to kill.[1] As you read the following stories drawn from newspaper reports, count the lives saved by armed self-defense.[2] Try to imagine what would have happened to the innocent citizens had they not been able to fight back.

## *Senior Shotgun Shooter Stops Axe Attackers*

Jim Dalton, 83, of Higbee, Missouri, was afraid that three men on his front porch were going to rob him, so he locked the door. He was proven correct when one of the men picked up an ax and started to hack his way through the door. Dalton armed himself, and when the men ignored his warnings and broke through the door, Dalton fired his shotgun, wounding one and routing all

---

[1]For many detailed and highly-readable accounts of lifesaving armed self-defense, see Robert A. Waters, *The Best Defense* (Cumberland House Publishing, 1998).

[2]Unless otherwise indicated, these stories are taken *verbatim* directly or adapted from "The Armed Citizen," a regular feature in the National Rifle Association's magazines *American Rifleman* and *American Guardian*. The NRA has graciously granted permission to quote and reproduce these accounts. The newspaper sources provided by the NRA magazines are cited in footnotes here for reference.

three. "I wouldn't prosecute a man who was defending his home from three ax-wielding hoodlums," said the local prosecutor.[3]

## Spunky Civilian Stops Kidnap, Rescues Child

"There's never a cop around when you need one," said Wayne Deal of Morgantown, North Carolina. When he saw a woman run from a building screaming that someone was stealing her car and kidnapping her son, Deal hopped in his car and took off in hot pursuit. After a half-mile chase, the criminal pulled over. "It looked like he'd pulled over to push the child out of the car," said Deal. "So I pulled up with my car and blocked him." Deal then retrieved the .22 pistol he legally carries in his car and, firing a warning shot, ordered the fleeing felon to stay put. Police arrived shortly and took the criminal into custody. The child was returned safely to his mother.[4]

## Nurse Stops Midnight Attacker in Bedroom

Alysha Jackson, a nurse in Baton Rouge, Louisiana, called the police often to complain about threats and harassment by her estranged husband. Eventually a court issued a restraining order against the man, but in the end it was a gun that saved Jackson from him. Returning from work at midnight, Jackson found her husband had broken into her apartment and was waiting for her. He physically restrained her, but she

---

[3]*The Daily Tribune*, Columbia, MO, March 11, 1994.

[4]*The Observer*, Charlotte, NC, June 15, 1994.

escaped. She found her gun and locked herself in the bedroom. When her husband kicked down the door, she shot him in the head, killing him. Police called the incident an obvious case of justifiable homicide.[5]

## Senior Lady Convinces Intruder To Scram

It was a hot night in Sacramento, so 80-year-old Lillian Carlson left her porch door open when she went to bed. This provided easy access for an intruder, who appeared in the bedroom. Carlson reached for the gun she had kept in her nightstand for 50 years, aimed it at her unwelcome guest, and said, "You can live or die. Which is it going to be?" The culprit walked out and then walked back in. Two shots from Carlson's antique revolver convinced him to leave for good. Police arrested a wounded suspect the next morning.[6]

## Quick Thinking and Quick-drawing Foil Robber

A Phoenix motorist stopping at a convenience store for gas got the feeling that something was wrong when a "clerk" told him to take all the gas he wanted. The real clerk was handcuffed on the floor behind the counter with a gun to his head. When he returned to his car, the alert customer got his gun and walked to a pay phone to call 911. Seeing this, the robber "clerk" exited the store and began firing at the customer. The

---

[5]*The Advocate*, Baton Rouge, LA, March 7, 1994.

[6]*The Bee*, Sacramento, CA, July 12, 1994.

customer returned fire, hitting his target in the shoulder. Police arrested the wounded criminal later.[7]

## Predator Bolts When
## Victim Pulls A .38

At 10:30 a.m., in broad daylight, a 35-year-old woman was getting out of her car in a parking lot in Montgomery, Alabama. Suddenly a man approached her from behind, knocked her unconscious, pushed her back into her car, and drove away with her. When she awoke, the abductor had driven her car into some woods. She struggled with him briefly, and then remembered the .38 revolver in her glove compartment. She managed to get it, shot twice and missed. The terrified kidnapper slammed on the brakes and bolted away on foot.[8]

## Young Teen Defends Brothers,
## Shoots Intruder

Four boys in Tulsa, Oklahoma, did just what their parents told them to do if they were ever home alone and in danger. When they heard someone trying to break down the front door, they went to their parents' room. There the oldest boy, 13, aimed his mother's .357 magnum revolver at the locked door while his brother dialed 911. The intruder entered the house, headed straight for the bedroom and tried to force the door open. The oldest brother fired one shot through the door, killing the criminal. Police found rubber gloves, a folding knife and a large screwdriver in the

[7]*The Arizona Republic*, Phoenix, AZ, May 15, 1994.

[8]*The Advertiser*, Montgomery, AL, July 11, 1994.

man's pockets. The boys' father said, "The firearms training the boys received probably saved their lives."[9]

## 80-year-old Tricks then Blasts Armed Carjacker

Eighty-year-old Louis Sylvester of Toulminville, Alabama, pulled into his driveway. In his car were his walker, which he needs to get around, and .38 caliber pistol. A young man brandishing a sawed-off .22 rifle approached Sylvester and demanded Sylvester's car. Sylvester told the hoodlum that he needed his walker to get out of his car, but reached instead for his gun, and shot the would-be carjacker, killing him.[10]

## Gunshots Save 4-year-old Girl From Vicious Dogs

In a sadly-common scenario, a four-year-old girl in Hampton, Virginia, was attacked by a pair of vicious dogs at a neighborhood playground. Fortunately, DuBois Duke, a neighbor, heard the child's screams. "I saw the little girl on the ground with one dog holding her neck and the other biting her thigh," said Duke. "They were ripping her apart." Duke loaded his pistol and raced outside, firing twice to scare the dogs. When they ran off, he rushed the girl to the hospital, where she received more than 40 stitches.[11]

---

[9]*The World*, Tulsa, OK, July 21, 1994.

[10]*The Register*, Mobile, AL, July 28, 1994.

[11]*Daily Press*, Newport News, VA, August 23, 1994.

## Quick-thinking Shooter
## Averts Arson-murder

A woman and her boyfriend were awakened rather rudely by the woman's ex-boyfriend, who was pouring gasoline on them and all over the apartment. Before the would-be arsonist could strike a match, the new boyfriend pulled his pistol and began firing, hitting the attacker twice.[12]

## One Armed Restarauteur
## Stops Four Armed Bandits

Through a one-way mirror installed in his Brooklyn, New York, restaurant, Oscar Palmer saw four armed men enter and begin to grab the money in the cash register. One of the armed men turned and pointed his gun at the mirror. Palmer responded immediately by firing four shots with his .38 revolver. One robber was killed and the three others fled. No charges were filed against Palmer.[13]

## The Siren Didn't Stop Him...
## the Firearm Did

Criminals had tried to break into Susan Kaleta's Winetka, California, home twice in the same year. So Kaleta installed an alarm system. The next time she heard someone trying to break in, she hit the "panic button" on the alarm and called 911. The intruder, undaunted by the screeching siren, found her in the bedroom with the phone to her ear and a gun in her

---

[12]*The Advertiser*, Montgomery, AL, September 5, 1994.

[13]*The New York Times*, New York, NY, September 10, 1994.

hand. He came toward her, so she fired twice, critically wounding him. Police said the intruder was responsible for the two earlier break-in attempts at Kaleta's home.[14]

## He Dialed 911, But His Pistol Saved His Life

An intruder who was burglarizing several units in a Philadelphia apartment building made a big mistake when he broke into Jack Arnold's place. The off-duty firefighter woke up when he heard banging on his front door. After calling 911, Arnold got his gun and hid in the bathroom. When the burglar broke down the front door, Arnold confronted him. The bandit raised a crowbar to strike Arnold, but Arnold fired two shots from his .32 caliber pistol, critically injuring the assailant. No charges were filed against Arnold.[15]

## Senior With Small .22 Pistol Stops Really Serious Burglar

After a man pounded on her door, cut the electric, telephone and alarm system lines to her house and launched several bricks through her windows, 61-year-old Annie Holt decided she'd had enough. With her .22 caliber derringer in hand, the Nashville resident repeatedly warned the harasser to stop trying to break in or else he would be shot. He didn't stop, so Holt finally shot and killed him.[16]

---

[14]*Daily News*, Los Angeles, CA, September 10, 1994.

[15]*The Philadelphia Inquirer*, Philadelphia, PA, August 31, 1994.

[16]*The Tennessean*, Nashville, TN, October 10, 1994.

## The Old "Pistol Under The Pillow" Trick

A wheelchair-bound 71-year-old Henrico County, Virginia, woman proved too tough for a local burglar. Lillian Allen kept a .32 caliber pistol under her pillow for special occasions. She was wheeling herself into the bedroom when she saw a criminal armed with a tire iron enter her home through the window. She got her gun and fired at the intruder, and he ran out the front door. The feisty grandmother said that she would not let crime drive her out of her neighborhood. "As long as I have the gun, I feel secure with that," she said.[17]

## 12-year-old Hunter Was Home Alone... With A 12-gauge

It was like a scene from the hit movie "Home Alone." A 12-year-old boy in Archer, Florida, used his wits, and a gun, to protect himself and his family's property. While the boy was watching TV, a burglar entered the farm house through an open side door. Seeing the intruder, the youngster retrieved the family's 12-gauge shotgun and fired one shot, sending the perpetrator packing. Reports indicated that the boy was an experienced hunter and familiar with firearms safety.[18]

## Teenage Girl Shows Her Gun To Peeping Tom

A 14-year-old girl was getting ready early one morning to go to her school in Plymouth Township,

---

[17]*The Richmond Times-Dispatch*, Richmond, VA, October 18, 1994.

[18]*The Sun*, Gainesville, FL, October 10, 1994.

Wisconsin, when she noticed a man peering inside through a bedroom window. The frightened girl, whose parents had already left for work, responded by getting a double barreled shotgun. That image was apparently enough to send the man fleeing. After the girl had reported seeing the same man the day before, her father had placed both the shotgun and a pistol within easy reach for just such a situation.[19]

## *Sixth Sense Warns, Handgun Saves Woman From Creep*

Tramona Crawford of Winston-Salem, North Carolina, was talking with her cousin on the telephone early one Thursday when a cold, shivering man appeared at her front door. The man told Crawford that his car had broken down and he needed to borrow some jumper cables. She hesitantly went to get the cables, but she also grabbed her gun from under her bed. Seconds later, the man burst through the door wielding a knife. Crawford shot him in self-defense, killing the invader. It happened that the man had been released from prison just two days earlier. Glad that her intuition had served her well, Crawford said, "I keep banging my head against the wall and asking myself, 'What if my instincts hadn't gone off?'"[20]

## *Armed Homeowner Captures Vicious Criminal For Police*

Fifty police and a Coast Guard helicopter had failed to find their man, but a Windsor, Connecticut,

---

[19]*The Janesville Gazette*, Janesville, WI, March 24, 1999.

[20]*The Charlotte Observer*, Charlotte, NC, March 31, 1999.

homeowner with a 9 mm pistol halted one criminal's day-long crime spree. The hunted fugitive had knifed and set an elderly man on fire, then kidnapped and raped the man's female companion. Jack O'Keefe, a retired engineer, discovered the criminal hiding in his car. While O'Keefe's wife dialed 911, O'Keefe held the thug at gun point until police arrived.[21]

## Woman Hiding In Bedroom Blasts Armed Bandits

Iron gates didn't stop a gang of armed invaders, but a .357 magnum pistol proved more effective for a woman in Las Vegas, Nevada. At least five burglars, some armed, rampaged through her upscale home while she hid in her bedroom. When one kicked down the locked bedroom door, she opened fire, wounding him and putting the other bandits to fight. The wounded criminal and four accomplices were later arrested.[22]

## Wife Dials 911 While Husband Operates .357

When Thedles Cannon, 71, first heard the crash, he thought a car had wrecked outside of his home in Wichita, Kansas. Then he realized an intruder had actually kicked in his front door. As his wife dialed 911, Cannon made his way downstairs with his .357 magnum pistol and confronted the burglar. When Cannon told him to "Freeze," the intruder instead

---

[21]*The Courant*, Hartford, CT, February 2, 1995.

[22]*Review-Journal*, Las Vegas, NV, February 11, 1995.

lunged at Cannon who then shot and seriously wounded the criminal.[23]

## Concealed Handgun Saves 108-year-old Tennessee Man

Maybe Richmond Watkins looked like easy prey to criminals. Watkins, believed to be Haywood County, Tennessee's oldest citizen at the time, was 108 years old. A crook 84 years younger tried to trick Watkins into thinking he owed some money for firewood. When the ruse didn't work, the younger man grew violent, put a butcher knife to Watkins' neck and threatened to kill him unless he handed over his money. Watkins reached into his pocket, but instead of a wallet he pulled out a .32 caliber handgun and shot the attacker in the neck.[24]

## Burgle Me Twice... You're History

The burglar evidently believed the first break-in of 57 year-old Floyd Williams' home had been such an easy job that he returned just over a week later to do it again. During the first incident, the suspect beat Williams with a pipe, laying a three-inch gash across his head. When the attacker returned, however, Williams was ready, armed with a .25 caliber pistol. As the intruder broke through the front door, the Lovington, New Mexico, homeowner fired and hit him in the leg. The wounded house-breaker ran to a car, and he and an accomplice fled the scene. Two months later police found the body of the fatally wounded

---

[23]*The Eagle*, Wichita, KS, January 11, 1995.

[24]*The States Graphic*, Brownsville, TN, June 13, 1996.

suspect in a ditch where the accomplice might have dumped it.[25]

## Gunning Grannies Teach Thugs Some Manners

Some folks in Grant County, Washington, called Marty Killinger, 61, and Dorothy Cunningham, 75, the "Pistol Packing Grandmas." No wonder. Four young thugs had cut the telephone lines and then forced their way into the women's rural home. As the punks struggled with Killinger in an attempt to get her car keys, Cunningham retrieved a Luger pistol from her bedroom and chased the intruders into the yard where they started taunting her. Cunningham fired several shots over the heads of the suspects who decided then to scram. "This is a clear message to criminals that senior citizens won't tolerate this type of behavior from these young punks," said Sheriff Bill Wiester later.[26]

## Armed Homeowner Ends Gang Rampage

Clad in dark-hooded sweatshirts and pants, a gang of armed men stormed a duplex in Rochester, New York. A neighboring homeowner witnessed the attack and grabbed his shotgun to defend his home and family. The roving band of marauders descended upon the his home and forced their way inside. The armed homeowner opened fire, trading shots with as many as seven of the men. Two of the attackers were killed and one was wounded as the homeowner successfully

---

[25]*The Avalanche-Journal*, Lubbock, TX, January 31, 1997.

[26]*The World*, Wenatchee, WA, February 16, 1997.

drove them out. Neighbors of the home defender were considering following his lead and arm themselves for protection. This decision was especially attractive to them because there had been previous home invasions that same summer which had left two citizens dead.[27]

## Citizen With Gun
## Rescues State Cop in Scuffle

Things had turned ugly for Oklahoma Highway Patrol Officer Rick Wallace. He had stopped a speeder and discovered the driver had marijuana, but the driver overpowered the officer. A passerby, Adolph Krejsek, witnessed the scuffle and came to the rescue, using his own firearm to help the trooper control the suspect. After helping subdue the assailant, Krejsek used the injured trooper's radio to call for help.[28]

## Still Awaiting 911 Response, Armed
## Resident Shoots Invading Prowler

The first time John Holsinger called the sheriff's office, he reported a prowler near his residence in Jackson, Ohio. While Holsinger was waiting for deputies to arrive, the crazed man started smashing windows on the home. Holsinger warned the man not to come inside. Disregarding the warnings the prowler forced his way through the front door. Holsinger then saw little choice but to shoot the housebreaker with a .22 caliber firearm. Eight minutes after his first call to

---

[27]*The Democrat and Chronicle*, Rochester, NY, August 27, 1997.

[28]*The Review Courier*, Alva, OK, January 8, 1995. Recounting this story here does not imply any endorsement of "drug laws."

the sheriff, Holsinger called back to report that he had shot the attacker.[29]

## Gun In Home Saves Dad, Mom & Baby

Jimmie Rogers initially had some concerns about bringing a new .380 pistol into the apartment where he lived with his infant daughter and fiancee. Two weeks later, he learned his decision had been correct. Rogers used the .380 pistol to scare a burglar out his home after finding the intruder just steps away from his daughter's bedroom. "I'm glad I had it," said Rogers about his firearm.[30]

## Armed Professional Woman Stops Rape, Then Chases Down Suspect

A female real estate agent in Stockton, California, thwarted an attempted rape with quick thinking and a .380 pistol. A man posing as a potential home buyer attacked her in a model home. She dropped to the floor, drew the pistol from her purse, and forced the man to flee. Back on her feet, she chased him outside and fired several shots at the man but missed him. She halted his escape by shooting out the tires of his car as he tried to drive away. With the help of some nearby construction workers, she held the thug for police.[31]

---

[29]*The Columbus Dispatch*, Columbus, OH, March 9, 1995

[30]*The News & Observer*, Raleigh, NC, February 25, 1995.

[31]*The Record*, Stockton, CA, February 18, 1995.

## Pistol-Packing Preacher Ends Robber's Religious Ruse

Deacon Bob McMillan grew suspicious of the 18-year-old man who had asked him to pray with him following services at a church in Apache Junction, Arizona. During a break in prayer, McMillan retrieved the .32 caliber pistol he kept in his car. Upon returning, his suspicions were confirmed. The deacon found the stranger waving a handgun at his wife's head and two others, demanding the weekly offerings. McMillan pushed his wife out of the way and quickly shot the man, wounding him. He then called the police. McMillan said later, "I felt I only had a split second to live."[32]

## When Lady with .357 Magnum Speaks, House Burglars Listen

After spotting a strange truck in the driveway of her Bell County, Kentucky, home, Darlene Craig stopped and confronted the two men she found in the process of stealing her television, VCR and other items. Craig used her .357 magnum revolver to even the playing field and forced both men to sit on the couch while she dialed 911. When one of the crooks pushed down the phone's receiver and said he didn't think the woman would shoot, Craig dared them to "give her a reason." The two men opted to wait for police.[33]

---

[32]*The Tribune,* Mesa, AZ, March 19, 1997.

[33]*The Enquirer,* Pineville, KY, April 4, 1996.

## "Disabled" Doesn't Mean "Defenseless"

Wheelchair-bound jeweler Scott Moline was alone in his store in West Allis, Wisconsin, when two customers-turned-bandits charged behind the counter. As one of the attackers drew a gun, Moline instinctively pulled his own .38 caliber handgun and loosed three shots. He missed, but the defense was enough to frighten the suspects. They ran away, leaving behind their own gun and their stolen get-away car parked out front. Police arrested the two suspects shortly later.[34]

## 911 Was Talking, But .44 Magnum Was Protecting Teen Girl

Despite the presence of her parents and a sheriff's deputy, a 15-year-old teenager was still forced to defend herself from an abusive ex-boyfriend. Confronted by the deputy and the girl's parents outside of the family's residence, the young man broke free from the deputy, jumped a fence, and kicked down the door of the house where the girl was hiding. Inside, the ex-boyfriend charged at the girl as she held the telephone in one hand—with a 911 operator on the line—and a Ruger .44 magnum revolver in the other hand. With a single shot the terrified girl terminated both the attack and the attacker.[35]

---

[34]*The Star*, West Allis, WI, May 23, 1996.

[35]*The Herald-Citizen*, Cookeville, TN, June 13, 1996.

## Hard-Working Immigrants "Just Say No" to Robbers

The American Dream doesn't come cheaply, and Samer and Khalid Mohd were not about to give up their part to a robber. The two immigrants ran a convenience store in downtown Miami, Florida, and kept a rifle close by for protection. Wearing a shirt as a mask and socks on his hands, a would-be robber entered the brothers' store holding a knife over his head and demanding money. Samer ran to the nearby office, grabbed his semi-automatic SKS rifle and used it to make the thief surrender. The two brothers held the bandit until police arrived. "They were too fast for me," the crook reportedly said.[36]

## Store Owner Ends One Criminal Career And Saves A Life

Nam Chun owned a convenience store in Orange County, Florida, and had been robbed four times. He determined not to be robbed again. When an armed and masked man entered Chun's store shortly after closing time and began beating one of the employees, Chun drew his own pistol and shot the attacker three times. The robber stumbled out the door to the parking lot where he died. Fellow store owners and patrons praised Chun for his decisive action.[37]

---

[36]*The Daily News*, Palatka, FL, August 8, 1997.

[37]*The Sentinel*, Orlando, FL, September 1, 1997.

## Handy Loaded Pistol Stops Knife-Swinging Attacker

After receiving threatening phone calls from a male acquaintance, a Virginia Beach, Virginia, woman feared she might be confronted by the man. One morning he appeared at her door under the pretense of retrieving a hair dryer he had lent the woman and her husband. She asked him to wait while she went to get the dryer and she shut the door. While she was in the bedroom, the man broke into the home, went to the kitchen and armed himself with a steak knife. The attacker confronted the woman and threatened her in the bedroom, where she pulled out her husband's semi-automatic pistol from a nightstand drawer. She warned him several times, but the attacker lunged at her anyway. She fired and hit him several times, killing him. It turned out that the attacker was a criminal out on bond.[38]

## Armed Lady Stops Three Felonious Punks

After her Carroll Valley, Pennsylvania, home was burglarized, Linda Steinle bought a .40 caliber pistol and took courses to learn how to safely use it. One morning she heard a screen being knocked out of a back window and, pistol in hand, she went to investigate. She found three teenagers discussing breaking into her home and getting ready to hot-wire the all-terrain vehicle (ATV) parked under her back deck. Steinle told the youths to freeze, and said, "Don't

---

[38]*The Virginian-Pilot*, Hampton Road, VA, September 11, 1997.

do anything stupid... I know how to use this." She led them into her home where she dialed 911 and held them for police. The three youths were charged with criminal conspiracy and attempted burglary.[39]

## Man Protects Wife and Baby From Two Armed Invaders

Although ailing from cancer, Mark Falletti successfully stopped two armed home invaders early one morning in his home in Boston, Massachusetts. The men had kicked in the front door of the apartment and had run upstairs towards the master bedroom. While his wife called 911, Falletti confronted the intruders with a pistol. When Falletti startled them and knocked one intruder's gun out of his hand, they fled. One tried to get back into the home to get the dropped gun, and Falletti shot him in the leg. The two attackers ran away again. When interviewed later, Falletti said he had acted to protect his seven-month-old son who had been asleep in his upstairs bedroom. "I did it because of the kid," he said.[40]

## Two Street Cleaners Successfully Refuse To Be Victims

Two street cleaners in Las Cruces, New Mexico, had been robbed before and decided to do something about it. So Ramon Zamora and Jesus Zavala obtained concealed carry permits for their 9 mm handguns. When accosted by three youths who brandished pistols and threatened to rob them, the two men drew their

---

[39]*The Times*, Gettysburg, PA, August 30, 1997.

[40]*The Boston Herald*, Boston, MA, July 24, 1997.

own guns and shot the three attackers. One attacker was killed, the other two were wounded. The authorities did not charge Zamora or Zavala with any crime.[41]

## Teenage Son With Shotgun Saves Dad

When two masked men entered a Houston, Texas, home and attacked the homeowner, his 15-year-old son grabbed a shotgun and opened fire. The men fled, but one collapsed outside the house and later died. Police did not file criminal charges against the boy.[42]

## Concealed-carry Revolver Stops Pummelers

As nurse Jim Shaver, 49, walked to his job early one morning in Eugene, Oregon, two men, ages 19 and 20, knocked him to the ground and began beating him in an apparent robbery attempt. Shaver, who was legally carrying a .22 revolver, twice warned the thugs that he was armed. Undaunted, they continued to assault him, so Shaver fired several shots, wounding one of the assailants. Both of them ran away.[43]

## Ninety-one years old and Disabled... Armed And Alive!

The sounds of shattering glass woke a 91-year-old disabled woman late one evening in her home in Charlotte, North Carolina. An intruder had apparently broken windows in both the bathroom and the living

---

[41]*Sun News*, Las Cruces, NM, October 12, 1997.

[42]*The Chronicle*, Houston, TX, October 14, 1997.

[43]*The Register Guard*, Eugene, OR, March 11, 1998.

room of the house. The woman fired three shots from the handgun, and the intruder ran away. Social service workers found the woman the following evening. She was down on the floor and unable to get up or move herself, but otherwise she was uninjured.[44]

## Womans Saves Self, Children From Attempted Murder

An argument between a man and a woman inside a Louisiana residence turned violent when the man allegedly doused the victim with gasoline and struck matches in an attempt to set her on fire. The woman swept up her two young children and fled the house, but her tormentor chased after her. Once at her car, the woman retrieved a handgun and held off the man so that she and her children could escape.[45]

## Wheelchair Is Just Another Position for Defensive Shooting

"I don't like to feel like a victim," said Rachel Jackson of Red Springs, North Carolina, after successfully running off an attacker who had broken into her home. Jackson, whose *spina bifida* condition confines her to a wheelchair, first sprayed the man with tear gas. Then, while the man went to grab money from her purse, Jackson pulled a .25 caliber pistol and fired four shots. The man was later caught while seeking treatment at a hospital. It turned out that he

[44]*The Charlotte Observer*, Charlotte, NC, May 9, 1998.
[45]*The Times-Picayune*, New Orleans, LA, August 4, 1998.

had been previously convicted of robbery, kidnapping and attempted rape.[46]

## *Crazed Criminal Loses Battle Against Blind Woman And Disabled Man*

A disabled man and a legally blind woman were in their Kalama, Washington, home one Friday afternoon when a 31-year-old man forced his way inside and jerked the disabled man to the floor. The invader was about to punch his victim when the blind woman started pulling on him from behind. As the invader slammed the blind woman against the wall, the disabled man grabbed a gun and forced the attacker to retreat outside. When the perpetrator was caught he admitted to his crime but could not give a reason for his action other than to say he'd had a bad couple of days.[47]

---

[46]*Fayetteville Observer-Times*, Fayetteville, NC, July 28, 1998.

[47]*The Daily News*, Longview, WA, May 1, 1999.

# What If 911 Breaks Down?

Most of the cases in this book involve government and police decisions about responding to and handling citizen emergencies. What happens if the citizen dials 911, but the 911 system does not work?

This is not a legal question. It is a practical question. It might be a life and death question.

## *System Is Down For Testing...*
## *Man Dies*

While conducting a "routine test of emergency generators," on January 31, 1999, technicians shut off power to the 911 center in Brooklyn, New York.[1] While the system was down, a 41-year-old man collapsed in his girlfriend's home. "I was holding him, talking to him and calling 911," she said. "I was calling 911, and I was getting a busy signal." She finally ran three blocks barefoot to the police station, but by the time help came, it was too late for the stricken man. He died of an apparent heart attack.

A backup system was supposed to forward 911 calls to police headquarters, but it had malfunctioned. On an average Sunday, the system receives 500 calls per hour at that time of morning. About 74 other medical calls had also gone unanswered during the down time.

---

[1]This story was reported by Donna De La Cruz, *Death Occurs During NYC 911 Failure*, Associated Press wire story, February 1, 1999.

## Y2K Threat To 911?

As of this writing (July 1999), many Americans fear problems caused by the "Y2K bug." In simplest terms, the "Y2K bug" refers to the troubles that some computer hardware and programs will experience when they try to process dates past December 31, 1999. The effect of the "Y2K bug" on a computer system could range from minor annoyances to catastrophic critical systems failure. Accordingly, business and governmental entities are working to repair any computer system that might suffer a serious problem as the century turns.

The National Association of Counties said on December 8, 1998, that "many county-run 911 emergency response systems risk an immobilizing computer failure on January 1, 2000, because half of the country's counties lack plans to deal with the Y2K problem."[2] The concern was that if the Y2K bug infected computerized emergency systems, the police, fire and ambulance services would be unable to receive or respond to citizen calls.

An April 29, 1999, news article reported that, according to one study, only 10 percent of all 911 reception points were prepared to operate properly when the year turned to 2000.[3] According to government officials, a recent Federal Communications Commission report indicated that the current Y2K readiness of 911 reception points might be as high as

---

[2]*Y2K problem could imperil 911 systems*, Associated Press, reported in the Seattle Times, December 8, 1998.

[3]Robert MacMillan, *911, Emergency Services Still Shaky on Y2K*, Newsbytes, April 29, 1999.

35 percent. Federal government authorities found that only 40 percent of the 911 reception points had contingency plans to handle the Y2K date problem.

Whether the "Y2K bug" will seriously affect 911 services is not known at this date. Yet it doesn't take a computer glitch to kill a 911 system. A failure of power or a break in telephone lines can occur at any time.

Of course a criminal attacker might simply cut the power and telephone lines of the intended victim's home. In such a case the victim could not dial 911 anyway. An otherwise defenseless person in such a case would chillingly prove the point: *you can dial 911... and die.*

# About the Author

Richard W. Stevens worked for nearly 10 years as a computer systems analyst, then began a new career after graduating *magna cum laude* from the University of San Diego School of Law in 1988. He practiced civil litigation in California, then for several years taught legal research and writing at George Washington University Law School and George Mason University School of Law. He currently specializes in preparing trial court motions and appellate court briefs in Washington, D.C.

His articles on a variety of subjects have appeared in legal and other publications, and he is editor of the *Firearms Sentinel,* a publication of Jews for the Preservation of Firearms Ownership. Mr. Stevens also edited, revised and fully annotated the book of *Standardized Civil Jury Instructions for the District of Columbia* (1998 edition). He has appeared frequently as a guest on radio and television talk shows to encourage all Americans to understand and celebrate the Bill of Rights.

All of these activities take second place behind his commitment to serving as husband and father to wife Connie and sons Andrew and Jason. The family now lives in Virginia and together they enjoy travel, water sports, winter sports, spirited conversation and fine dining.

# What Others Say About
## *Dial 911 and Die*

### *Completely Indispensable*

*Dial 911 and Die* is a book that should have been written a long time ago. The enormity of the facts its author, attorney Richard Stevens, reveals is almost too much to take in. The notion that the police have no legal obligation in most instances to protect the life, property, and rights of any given individual—while at the same time spending unthinkable amounts of time and energy attempting to deprive that individual of the means and legal right to self-defense—puts the lie to every claim for government that statists have ever made.

The remedy—a general reassertion of that right—is the only rational response to the facts that Stevens presents state by state. His book may even set the stage for something truly revolutionary, perhaps even repeal of the pernicious and un-American Doctrine of Sovereign Immunity on which these more specific official evasions of responsibility rely.

There are only four or five Completely Indispensable books in the world. Richard Stevens has managed to add another one to their number.

L. Neil Smith
Author of *The Probability Broach*,
*Pallas*, and *The Mitzvah*
(with Aaron Zelman)

### Required Reading

*Dial 911 and Die* is a book that will open your eyes - and possibly even save your life, or the life of someone you love. It should be required reading for anyone who doesn't realize that he has primary, if not sole, responsibility for protecting and defending himself.

*Dial 911 and Die* presents a compelling argument for restoring the individual right of self-defense. But it's also a compelling argument for reforming, if not revoking, the legal doctrines of "sovereign immunity" and "public duty," or for privatizing emergency services.

While government has no duty to protect people, or even to prevent crime and apprehend criminals, it has arrogated to itself the power to disarm them.

Isn't it interesting that a person is a "responsible citizen" if he keeps a cell phone, a fire extinguisher, and a first aid kit handy, but is presumed to be a criminal if he keeps a loaded firearm available for self-defense?

Buy this book for friends and relatives who still believe the police will protect them. If it saves just one life, it's worth it!

Sarah Thompson, MD
Writer and liberty activist
*http://www.therighter.com*

### Tremendous Research

How I wish that the information in this book were not true. Nevertheless, this book speaks to the irrefutable truth: *police do very little to prevent violent crime*. We investigate crime after the fact. I applaud Richard Stevens for his tremendous research and his courage to tell this truth.

> Richard Mack
> Former Sheriff of Graham County, Arizona

---

### A Sobering Heads-up

For those good-hearted citizens who believe the police should and will protect them and their families, *Dial 911 and Die* is a sobering heads-up. Nowhere in our nation do the police have the duty or the capability to protect most of Americans. *Dial 911 and Die* documents the case law and statutes that drive home that we are responsible for protecting ourselves and our loved ones.

> Edgar A. Suter, MD
> National Chair, Doctors for
> Integrity in Policy Research Inc.
> *http://www.dipr.org*

### *Think Again*

If you thought the police were required to protect you from violent crime, then think again. Stevens' book dramatically explains the legal reality behind the title *Dial 911 and Die.*

> Larry Pratt
> Executive Director,
> Gun Owners of America
> *http://www.gunowners.org*